Unlocking the Secrets of the Ouija Board: Gateway to the Unknown or Product of Suggestion?

LUNA WOLFHEART

Chapter 1: Introduction

The Ouija board is a mysterious and controversial object that has captured the public's imagination for over a century. From its humble beginnings as a parlor game in the late 19th century to its current status as a tool for contacting the dead, the Ouija board has fascinated and frightened countless individuals.

But what exactly is a Ouija board, and why has it stirred up so much controversy? In this book, we will explore the history, science, and spiritual aspects of the Ouija board, as well as the personal experiences and opinions of those who have used it.

Whether you're a skeptic or a believer, a seasoned user or someone who has never touched a Ouija board, this book will provide you with a comprehensive understanding of this enigmatic tool. Join us as we journey into the world of the Ouija board and uncover its secrets.

Explanation of what a Ouija board is

A Ouija board is a flat board usually made of wood, plastic, or cardboard that is inscribed with the letters of the alphabet, numbers 0 through 9, and various words and symbols such as "yes," "no," and "goodbye." It is used as a tool for divination, allowing users to communicate with spirits, ghosts, or other entities from the other side.

The board typically comes with a small heart-shaped or triangular pointer, called a planchette, that is placed on the board and moves around to spell out messages. Users place their fingers on the planchette and ask questions, with the belief that the spirits will move the planchette to answer them.

The origins of the Ouija board can be traced back to the spiritualist movement of the late 19th century, which sought to communicate with the dead. The board was originally marketed as a parlor game, but its association with the supernatural soon grew, leading to its use in seances and other occult practices.

Today, Ouija boards are still sold in many toy and game stores and are used by people of all ages and backgrounds. Some use them for entertainment, while others use them in more serious contexts such as paranormal investigations or as a means of contacting deceased loved ones.

Despite their widespread popularity, Ouija boards remain a controversial and polarizing topic, with some people claiming that they are harmless tools for spiritual exploration while others warn of the dangers of using them. The debate continues to this day, making the Ouija board a fascinating and intriguing subject for exploration.

Brief history of the Ouija board

The Ouija board has a long and storied history that dates back to the late 19th century. Its origins can be traced to the spiritualist movement, which was popular at the time and sought to communicate with the dead. Spiritualism gained widespread popularity in the wake of the Civil War, when many people were grieving for loved ones who had been killed in battle.

In 1890, businessman Elijah Bond patented the first Ouija board, which was then marketed as a parlor game. The board was made of wood and featured the letters of the alphabet, numbers, and various symbols. It also came with a small planchette that users placed their fingers on in order to spell out messages from spirits.

The Ouija board quickly gained popularity and became a sensation across the United States, with people holding seances and using the board to communicate with the dead. In 1901, the rights to the Ouija board were purchased by William Fuld, who improved the design and mass-produced it. The board became a household name, and Fuld even claimed that the name "Ouija" was derived from an ancient Egyptian word meaning "good luck. »

During the early 20th century, the Ouija board continued to be used for both entertainment and spiritual purposes, with some people claiming that they had received messages from deceased loved ones or other entities from the beyond. However, the board also began to attract controversy, with some religious groups and skeptics warning of its potential dangers and the possibility of demonic possession.

Despite the controversy, the Ouija board continued to be a popular item and has remained so to this day. It has inspired countless books, movies, and TV shows and has become a cultural icon in its own right. Whether it's viewed as a harmless parlor game or a dangerous tool for contacting the dead, the Ouija board remains a fascinating and intriguing object that has captured the public's imagination for over a century.

The controversy surrounding the use of Ouija boards

The use of Ouija boards has been a subject of controversy and debate for many years. While some people view them as harmless tools for communicating with the dead or exploring the supernatural, others believe that they can be dangerous and even demonic.

One of the main concerns surrounding the use of Ouija boards is the possibility of opening oneself up to negative or malevolent spirits. Some people believe that the board can act as a portal for negative energies or entities, and that using it can result in demonic possession or other negative consequences. This belief is often rooted in religious or spiritual traditions that view the practice of communicating with spirits as dangerous or taboo.

Another concern is the potential for psychological harm. Some people argue that using a Ouija board can lead to paranoia, anxiety, or even mental illness, particularly if the user becomes obsessed with the board or the messages they receive through it. This belief is often based on the idea that the board can tap into subconscious or repressed thoughts and feelings, which can be distressing or traumatic for some people.

There are also skeptics who dismiss the use of Ouija boards as mere superstition or a form of self-deception. They argue that any messages or information received through the board can be attributed to the ideomotor effect, in which the user unconsciously moves the planchette in response to their own expectations or desires.

The use of Ouija boards remains popular among many people who view them as a means of spiritual exploration or entertainment. Whether they are viewed as harmless games or dangerous tools, the Ouija board continues to be a topic of fascination and debate in popular culture.

Chapter 2: How to use a Ouija board

Before using a Ouija board, it's important to understand how it works and the proper steps for using it safely and effectively. While some people may view the board as a simple parlor game, others believe that it can be a powerful tool for communicating with the dead or exploring the supernatural.

In this chapter, we'll take a closer look at how to use a Ouija board. We'll cover the basic steps for setting up the board, choosing a partner, and initiating communication with the spirits. We'll also discuss some of the potential risks and pitfalls of using the board, and provide tips for staying safe and protecting yourself from negative energies or entities.

Whether you're a curious beginner or an experienced user, this chapter will provide you with the knowledge and tools you need to use a Ouija board with confidence and care. So grab your board, gather your friends, and get ready to explore the mysterious and fascinating world of the Ouija board.

Step-by-step instructions on how to use a Ouija board

- Choose a quiet, dimly lit room for your session. Turn off any electronics or distractions, such as phones or televisions.

- Gather your materials. You'll need a Ouija board, a planchette (the small, heart-shaped piece that moves across the board), and at least one partner to use the board with.

- Decide on your intention for the session. Are you seeking to communicate with a specific spirit or entity? Or are you simply curious to see if the board works? It's important to have a clear intention before beginning your session.

- Sit across from your partner and place the board on a flat surface between you. Place the planchette in the center of the board.

- Both you and your partner should place your fingers lightly on the planchette. Close your eyes and take a few deep breaths to relax and focus.

- Begin by asking the board if any spirits are present and would like to communicate. Wait for a response, which may come in the form of the planchette moving on its own or spelling out words.

- Once you have established communication with a spirit, ask questions and wait for a response. Remember to remain respectful and courteous, and avoid asking personal or invasive questions.

- If you feel uncomfortable or uneasy at any point during the session, immediately end the session and say goodbye to the spirit.

- When you are ready to end the session, say goodbye to the spirit and move the planchette to "Goodbye" on the board. Thank the spirit for communicating with you and end the session with a prayer or positive affirmation.

It's important to note that using a Ouija board can be a powerful and potentially dangerous experience. It's important to approach the board with respect and caution, and to protect yourself from negative energies or entities. Always end the session with a positive intention and say goodbye to any spirits you have communicated with.

Precautions to take before using a Ouija board

Know your purpose:

Knowing your purpose before using a Ouija board is essential for creating a positive and safe experience. Before using the Ouija board, it's important to identify why you want to communicate with spirits and what you hope to achieve from the session.

- Set your intention: Before starting the session, set your intention for using the Ouija board. Ask yourself why you want to communicate with spirits and what you hope to achieve from the session.

- Identify your motivation: Ask yourself what motivates you to use the Ouija board. Are you seeking guidance, closure, or simply a connection to the spiritual world? Understanding your motivation can help you stay focused during the session.

- Be clear on your boundaries: It's important to set clear boundaries before using the Ouija board. This includes identifying which types of spirits you are willing to communicate with and what topics are off-limits. Setting clear boundaries can help protect you from negative or harmful energies.

- Visualize positive outcomes: Visualize positive outcomes for the session, such as receiving guidance, healing, or closure. By focusing on positive outcomes, you can promote a positive and peaceful environment for communication.

- Respect the process: Remember to respect the process and avoid forcing communication. It's important to allow spirits to communicate at their own pace and to be patient and respectful throughout the session.

Knowing your purpose before using a Ouija board can help you stay focused and create a positive and safe experience. By setting clear intentions, identifying your motivation, and visualizing positive outcomes, you can promote positive energy and enhance your communication with spirits.

Write down your intentions:

Writing down your intentions before using a Ouija board can help you stay focused and maintain a positive and safe environment for communication. When you write down your intentions, you create a physical reminder of your purpose and goals for the session, which can help you stay on track and avoid distractions.

Here are some tips on how to write down your intentions before using a Ouija board:

- Be specific: When writing down your intentions, be as specific as possible about what you hope to achieve from the session. This can include the types of spirits you want to communicate with, the topics you want to discuss, or the specific guidance or healing you seek.

- Use positive language: Use positive language when writing down your intentions. This can help promote positive energy and create a more conducive environment for communication.

- Keep it simple: Keep your intentions simple and focused. Avoid trying to address too many topics at once, as this can make it difficult to stay focused and may lead to confusion or frustration.

- Review and revise: Review your intentions before starting the session, and make any necessary revisions or adjustments. This can help ensure that your intentions are clear and aligned with your purpose for the session.

- Visualize positive outcomes: Visualize positive outcomes as you write down your intentions. This can help you stay focused and promote a positive and peaceful environment for communication.

Writing down your intentions before using a Ouija board can help you stay focused, maintain a positive environment for communication, and achieve your goals for the session. By being specific, using positive language, keeping it simple, reviewing and revising, and visualizing positive outcomes, you can enhance your communication with spirits and promote a positive and safe experience.

Visualize your intentions:

Visualization is a powerful technique that can help you focus your energy and intentions before using a Ouija board. When you visualize your intentions, you create a mental picture of what you hope to achieve, which can help you manifest your desires and promote positive energy for communication.

Here are some tips on how to visualize your intentions before using a Ouija board:

- Relax and clear your mind: Find a quiet and peaceful space where you can relax and clear your mind. Take a few deep breaths and focus on your breath to calm your mind and body.

- Visualize your intentions: Close your eyes and visualize your intentions. Imagine yourself achieving your desired outcome, such as communicating with a specific spirit, receiving guidance or healing, or gaining clarity on a specific topic.

- Use all your senses: Use all your senses to create a vivid and detailed mental picture. Imagine what it feels like to achieve your desired outcome, what you see, hear, smell, and touch.

- Maintain a positive mindset: As you visualize your intentions, maintain a positive mindset and focus on positive outcomes. Avoid negative thoughts or doubts that can disrupt your energy and intentions.

- Repeat positive affirmations: Repeat positive affirmations that support your intentions, such as "I am open to positive communication with spirits" or "I trust that I will receive the guidance I need. »

Visualizing your intentions before using a Ouija board can help you focus your energy, manifest your desires, and promote positive communication with spirits. By relaxing and clearing your mind, using all your senses, maintaining a positive mindset, and repeating positive affirmations, you can enhance your visualization practice and promote a positive and safe experience.

Use positive language:

Using positive language is an important aspect of preparing to use a Ouija board. Positive language can help you set a clear intention for communication and promote a positive energy that can attract positive spirits and messages.
Here are some tips on how to use positive language before using a Ouija board:

- Avoid negative words: Avoid using negative words or phrases that can attract negative energies, such as "evil," "demon," or "harm." Instead, use positive words and phrases that promote love, light, and positive communication.

- Focus on your desired outcome: Use positive language to focus on your desired outcome. For example, instead of saying "I don't want to talk to any negative spirits," say "I intend to communicate with positive spirits who will bring me guidance and clarity. »

- Use affirmations: Use positive affirmations to reinforce your intentions and promote positive energy. Some examples of affirmations you can use before using a Ouija board include "I am open to positive communication with spirits," "I trust that I will receive messages that serve my highest good," or "I am surrounded by love and light. »

- Speak with conviction: When stating your intentions or affirmations, speak with conviction and believe in the power of your words. Your energy and mindset can greatly influence the outcome of your communication with spirits.

By using positive language before using a Ouija board, you can set a clear intention for positive communication and promote a safe and respectful environment for spirits to communicate with you. Remember to always approach the Ouija board with respect and intention, and to focus on positive outcomes that serve your highest good.

Speak your intentions out loud:

Speaking your intentions out loud before using a Ouija board can be a powerful way to set a clear intention for positive communication and to promote a safe and respectful environment for spirits to communicate with you. When you speak your intentions out loud, you give voice and energy to your desires, which can help to manifest them more effectively.
Here are some tips on how to speak your intentions out loud:

- Be clear and specific: When stating your intentions, be clear and specific about what you want to achieve. Avoid vague or ambiguous language that can create confusion or misinterpretation.

- Use positive language: As I mentioned earlier, using positive language can promote a positive energy and attract positive spirits and messages. Use positive words and phrases that promote love, light, and positive communication.

- Speak with conviction and belief: When you speak your intentions out loud, speak with conviction and belief in the power of your words. Your energy and mindset can greatly influence the outcome of your communication with spirits.

- Repeat your intentions: Repeat your intentions several times to reinforce them and help them sink into your subconscious mind. This can help you stay focused and aligned with your desired outcome throughout the Ouija board session.

Remember that speaking your intentions out loud is just one aspect of preparing to use a Ouija board. It's important to take all necessary precautions, such as choosing a safe location, using positive affirmations, and focusing on your desired outcome, to promote a safe and respectful environment for spirits to communicate with you.

Trust the process:

Trusting the process is an essential part of using a Ouija board effectively. When you trust the process, you allow yourself to be open to the messages and insights that come through the board, without doubting or questioning their validity. Here are some tips on how to trust the process when using a Ouija board:

- Let go of expectations: When you have specific expectations about what you want to achieve or what messages you want to receive, you may unconsciously block the flow of communication. Instead, approach the Ouija board session with an open mind and heart, and trust that the messages you receive will be for your highest good.

- Stay focused and centered: It's important to stay focused and centered during the Ouija board session, as distractions and external factors can interfere with the communication. Take deep breaths, relax your body, and clear your mind before starting the session.

- Avoid forcing the planchette: When you try to force the planchette to move in a certain direction or to spell out specific words, you may unknowingly influence the messages that come through the board. Instead, allow the planchette to move freely and organically, and trust that the messages will come through in their own way and time.

- Validate the messages: When you receive messages through the Ouija board, validate them by asking for clarification or confirmation. This can help you understand the meaning and relevance of the messages, and build trust in the communication process.

Remember that trust is a key component of effective communication with spirits through the Ouija board. By letting go of expectations, staying focused and centered, avoiding forcing the planchette, and validating the messages, you can establish a strong sense of trust and openness with the spirits that come through the board.

By setting clear intentions, you can create a focused and positive energy for your Ouija board session. This can help reduce the risk of negative entities and ensure a safe and positive experience.

Choose a safe location:

Choosing a safe location is another important step to take before using a Ouija board.

Here are some tips on how to choose a safe location:

• Choose a quiet, private location:

Choosing a quiet and private location is important when using a Ouija board because it creates a safe and focused environment for communication with spirits. Here are some things to consider when choosing a location:

- Avoid distractions: Choose a location that is free from distractions, such as loud noises, bright lights, or interruptions from other people. This will help you maintain a clear and focused connection with the spirits that come through the board.

- Create a comfortable environment: Set up the location in a way that feels comfortable and inviting to you. This may include using soft lighting, comfortable seating, and soothing music to create a peaceful atmosphere.

- Choose a private space: It's important to choose a location that is private and free from unwanted interruptions. This will help you feel safe and secure during the Ouija board session, and allow you to focus fully on the communication with spirits.

- Consider the energy of the location: Before using a Ouija board in a particular location, it's important to consider the energy of the space. Avoid using the board in locations that feel negative or unsettling, as this may interfere with the communication process.

By choosing a quiet and private location, you can create a safe and focused environment for using the Ouija board. This will allow you to establish a strong connection with the spirits that come through the board, and receive clear and meaningful messages.

• Avoid public spaces:

It's important to avoid using a Ouija board in public spaces, as this can be distracting and potentially unsafe. Here are some reasons why it's best to use a Ouija board in a private location rather than a public one:

- Distractions: Public spaces are often noisy and busy, with lots of people moving around and creating distractions. This can make it difficult to focus on the communication with spirits and receive clear messages.

- Safety concerns: Using a Ouija board in a public space can attract unwanted attention and potentially lead to unsafe situations. It's best to use the board in a quiet and private location where you feel safe and secure.

- Respect for others: Using a Ouija board in public spaces can be disrespectful to others who may not share your beliefs or feel uncomfortable with the activity. It's important to be respectful of others and avoid causing any unnecessary discomfort or disturbance.

- Interference with spirits: Public spaces are often filled with a lot of energy and activity, which can interfere with the communication with spirits. By using the board in a private location, you can minimize outside interference and create a more focused and meaningful connection with the spirits.

It's best to use a Ouija board in a private location where you feel safe and comfortable. This will allow you to create a peaceful and focused environment for communication with spirits, and receive clear and meaningful messages.

• Ensure proper lighting:

Proper lighting is important when using a Ouija board, as it can create a calming and peaceful atmosphere and help you focus on the communication with spirits. Here are some tips for ensuring proper lighting when using a Ouija board:

- Use dim lighting: It's best to use dim lighting when using a Ouija board, as this can create a relaxing and calming atmosphere. Avoid using bright overhead lights, which can be harsh and distracting.

- Use candles: Candles can provide a soft and calming light that is perfect for using a Ouija board. They can also create a soothing ambiance and help you relax.

- Use a small lamp: If you don't want to use candles, a small lamp with a soft, warm light can be a good alternative. Place the lamp near the board to create a focused and calming environment.

- Avoid using flashlights: Flashlights can create a harsh and jarring light that can be distracting and interfere with the communication with spirits. If you need additional light, use a dim lamp or candles instead.

- Choose a location with natural light: If possible, choose a location with natural light, such as a room with a window. This can provide a soft and calming light that is perfect for using a Ouija board.

Ensuring proper lighting is essential when using a Ouija board. By using dim lighting, candles, or a small lamp, you can create a calming and peaceful atmosphere that is conducive to communication with spirits.

• Remove any distractions:

When using a Ouija board, it's important to remove any distractions that could interfere with the communication with spirits. Here are some tips for removing distractions:

- Turn off electronic devices: Electronic devices such as cell phones, computers, and televisions can be very distracting when using a Ouija board. Turn off these devices or put them in another room to avoid any interruptions.

- Close doors and windows: Outside noises such as traffic or barking dogs can be distracting when using a Ouija board. Close doors and windows to reduce any outside noise.

- Choose a quiet time of day: Choose a time of day when the house or building is quiet and there are fewer distractions. Avoid using the Ouija board during busy times of day or when there are a lot of people around.

- Use headphones: If there are noises that cannot be avoided, such as construction work or loud neighbors, consider using noise-cancelling headphones to block out the noise.

- Set boundaries with others: If you are using the Ouija board with others, set boundaries beforehand. Let them know that you want to limit distractions and create a focused environment for communication with spirits.

Removing distractions is crucial when using a Ouija board. By minimizing outside noise and limiting distractions from electronic devices, you can create a peaceful and focused environment that is conducive to communication with spirits.

• Cleanse the space:

Before using a Ouija board, it is important to cleanse the space to remove any negative energy or entities that may be present. Here are some tips for cleansing the space:

- Burn sage: Sage smudging is a popular method for cleansing a space. Light a bundle of dried sage and let the smoke fill the room, making sure to focus on the corners and other areas where negative energy may be present.

- Use incense: Burning incense can also help to cleanse the space. Choose a scent that you find calming and light it before using the Ouija board.

- Ring a bell or chime: Ringing a bell or chime can help to clear any negative energy from the space. Start at one end of the room and move around the space, ringing the bell or chime as you go.

- Use crystals: Certain crystals, such as black tourmaline and amethyst, are known for their cleansing properties. Place these crystals around the room to help cleanse the space.

- Play calming music: Soft, calming music can help to create a peaceful and positive atmosphere, which can in turn help to cleanse the space.

Cleansing the space before using a Ouija board can help to create a more positive and focused environment for communication with spirits. By removing negative energy and entities, you can create a safer and more comfortable space for your Ouija board session.

• Set up a protective barrier:

In addition to cleansing the space, setting up a protective barrier can help to ensure a safe and positive Ouija board experience. Here are some tips for setting up a protective barrier:

- Visualize a protective shield: Close your eyes and visualize a white or golden protective shield surrounding you and anyone else participating in the Ouija board session. Imagine the shield as a powerful force that will keep out any negative energy or entities.

- Call on protective spirits: You can also call on protective spirits or entities to help set up a barrier. Some people like to call on angels, spirit guides, or other positive entities for protection.

- Use protective symbols: Certain symbols, such as the pentagram or the Eye of Horus, are believed to have protective properties. You can draw these symbols on a piece of paper and place them on the table where you will be using the Ouija board.

- Burn protective herbs: Burning herbs such as rosemary or lavender can help to create a protective barrier around the space. Simply light the herbs and let the smoke fill the room.

- Set intentions for protection: Before beginning the Ouija board session, set clear intentions for protection. You can state your intentions out loud, asking for protection from any negative entities or energies.

By setting up a protective barrier, you can create a sense of safety and security during your Ouija board session. Remember to stay focused on positive energy and intentions throughout the session, and to close the session properly when you are finished.

By choosing a safe location, you can create a comfortable and positive environment for your Ouija board session. This can help reduce distractions and ensure a safe and positive experience.

Invite positive energies:

Inviting positive energies is another important step to take before using a Ouija board. Here are some tips on how to invite positive energies:

State your intention to only communicate with positive energies:

Stating your intention to only communicate with positive energies is an important step to take before using a Ouija board. By setting clear intentions, you can ensure that you are only inviting positive and loving energies into the session.
Here are some tips on how to state your intention:

- Be specific: Be specific about your intention to communicate only with positive energies. State your intention clearly and firmly.

- Use positive language: Use positive language when stating your intention. Avoid using negative language, which can attract negative energies. For example, instead of saying "I don't want to communicate with negative energies", say "I only want to communicate with positive and loving energies ».

- Visualize positive outcomes: Visualize positive outcomes for the session. Imagine that you are surrounded by love and light, and that only positive and loving energies are welcome in the session.

- Focus on your intention: Focus on your intention throughout the session. Keep your intention at the forefront of your mind, and do not waver from it.

- Trust your intuition: Trust your intuition when communicating with the board. If you feel that negative energies are present, immediately end the session and cleanse the space.

By stating your intention to only communicate with positive energies, you can create a safe and positive environment for your Ouija board session. This can help promote positive communication and reduce the risk of attracting negative energies.

• Visualize positive energy:

Visualizing positive energy is a powerful technique that can help you invite positive energies into your Ouija board session. By visualizing positive energy, you can create a positive and loving atmosphere, which can promote positive communication and reduce the risk of attracting negative energies.
Here are some tips on how to visualize positive energy:

- Close your eyes: Close your eyes and take a few deep breaths. Focus on your breath and allow your body to relax.

- Visualize a bright light: Visualize a bright light surrounding you and your space. Imagine the light filling the room with love and positivity.

- Focus on the light: Focus your attention on the light and allow it to fill your body with positive energy. Imagine the light flowing through your body, filling every cell with positivity and love.

- Hold the visualization: Hold the visualization for a few minutes, allowing the positive energy to flow through you and your space.

- Repeat positive affirmations: While visualizing the positive energy, repeat positive affirmations to reinforce the visualization. For example, you can say "I am surrounded by love and positivity" or "Only positive and loving energies are welcome here ».

By visualizing positive energy, you can create a welcoming and positive environment for your Ouija board session. This can help promote positive communication and reduce the risk of attracting negative energies.

Call on spirit guides or angels:

Calling on spirit guides or angels is another way to invite positive energy into your Ouija board session. Spirit guides and angels are believed to be entities that are here to help and protect us. By calling on them, you can ask for their guidance and protection during the session.

Here are some tips on how to call on spirit guides or angels:

- Set your intention: Before calling on spirit guides or angels, set your intention to only communicate with positive energies.

- Close your eyes: Close your eyes and take a few deep breaths. Focus on your breath and allow your body to relax.

- Ask for protection: Ask your spirit guides or angels to protect you and your space during the session. You can say something like "I call on my spirit guides and angels to protect me and my space during this session ».

- Ask for guidance: Ask your spirit guides or angels to provide guidance during the session. You can say something like "I ask my spirit guides and angels to guide me towards positive and loving communication during this session ».

- Be open to receiving guidance: Be open to receiving guidance from your spirit guides or angels. Trust that they are there to help and protect you, and that they will provide you with the guidance you need.

By calling on spirit guides or angels, you can invite positive and loving energies into your Ouija board session. This can help promote positive communication and reduce the risk of attracting negative energies.

Use positive affirmations:

Using positive affirmations is another technique that can help you invite positive energies into your Ouija board session. Affirmations are positive statements that can help you shift your mindset and attract positive energy.
Here are some tips on how to use positive affirmations:

- Choose positive affirmations: Choose positive affirmations that resonate with you and your intentions for the session. For example, you can use affirmations such as "I am surrounded by love and positivity" or "I only communicate with positive and loving energies ».

- Repeat affirmations: Repeat your affirmations either silently or out loud before and during the session. This can help reinforce your intention to only communicate with positive energies.

- Believe in the affirmations: Believe in the power of your affirmations. Trust that by repeating positive affirmations, you are attracting positive energy and promoting positive communication.

- Stay focused: Stay focused on your affirmations throughout the session. This can help you stay centered and positive, even if you encounter negative energy or experiences.

By using positive affirmations, you can shift your mindset and attract positive energy into your Ouija board session. This can help promote positive communication and reduce the risk of attracting negative energies.

Burn candles or incense:

Burning candles or incense is a common practice that can help you create a positive and peaceful atmosphere during your Ouija board session. Burning candles or incense can help you relax and create a calming environment, which can be conducive to positive communication.

Here are some tips on how to use candles or incense during your Ouija board session:

- Choose candles or incense: Choose candles or incense that resonate with your intention for the session. For example, you can use lavender-scented candles or incense to promote relaxation and peace.

- Set up the candles or incense: Set up the candles or incense in a safe location, away from any flammable objects. You can also use candle holders or incense burners to contain the flames or ashes.

- Light the candles or incense: Light the candles or incense before you begin the session. Take a moment to focus on your intention and visualize positive energy surrounding you.

- Keep an eye on the candles or incense: Keep an eye on the candles or incense throughout the session to ensure they are burning safely. Do not leave the candles or incense unattended.

- Extinguish the candles or incense: Extinguish the candles or incense once you have completed the session. Use a candle snuffer or wet cloth to extinguish the flames.

By burning candles or incense during your Ouija board session, you can create a positive and peaceful environment that is conducive to positive communication. This can help promote positive energy and reduce the risk of attracting negative energies.

Use crystals:

Using crystals is another technique that can help you promote positive energy during your Ouija board session. Crystals are believed to have healing properties and can be used to amplify positive energy and protect against negative energy. Here are some tips on how to use crystals during your Ouija board session:

- Choose crystals: Choose crystals that resonate with your intention for the session. For example, clear quartz is a powerful crystal for amplifying positive energy, while amethyst can promote relaxation and protection.

- Cleanse the crystals: Cleanse the crystals before using them by placing them in salt water or smudging them with sage. This can help remove any negative energy that may be attached to the crystals.

- Set up the crystals: Set up the crystals around the Ouija board or in a grid formation to create a protective barrier. You can also hold the crystals in your hand during the session to promote positive energy.

- Visualize positive energy: Visualize positive energy surrounding you and the crystals. Focus on your intention and visualize the crystals amplifying positive energy and protecting you from negative energy.

- Cleanse the crystals after the session: Cleanse the crystals after the session to remove any negative energy that may have accumulated during the session.

Using crystals during your Ouija board session can help promote positive energy and protect against negative energy. By using crystals that resonate with your intention for the session, you can amplify positive energy and promote a positive and peaceful environment for communication.

By inviting positive energies, you can create a welcoming and safe space for your Ouija board session. This can help promote positive communication and reduce the risk of attracting negative energies.

Use a protective talisman:

Using a protective talisman is another way to create a protective barrier around yourself during a Ouija board session. Here are some tips for choosing and using a protective talisman:

Choose a talisman:

Choosing a talisman for protection during a Ouija board session is a personal decision, as different objects may hold different meanings and energies for different individuals. Here are some common types of talismans and their protective properties:

- Crystals: Certain crystals are believed to have protective properties and can be used as talismans. For example, black tourmaline is believed to protect against negative energies and psychic attacks, while amethyst is believed to protect against spiritual attacks and psychic vampires.

- Amulets: An amulet is a small object, often worn as jewelry, that is believed to have protective properties. Some common protective amulets include the evil eye, the Hamsa, and the Celtic knot.

- Symbols: Certain symbols are believed to have protective properties, such as the pentagram, which is commonly used in Wiccan and Pagan traditions, and the cross, which is commonly used in Christian traditions.

- Personal items: A personal item, such as a piece of jewelry that holds sentimental value, can also be used as a talisman. The item should be cleansed and charged with protective energy before use.

When choosing a talisman, it's important to select one that resonates with your personal beliefs and intentions. You can also consider the properties of different stones, symbols, and amulets to find one that aligns with your desired level of protection. Remember to cleanse and charge your talisman before use, and set clear intentions for it to provide protection during the Ouija board session.

• Cleanse the talisman:

Cleansing the talisman is an important step to ensure that it is free of any negative energies or vibrations that could interfere with its protective properties. Here are some common methods for cleansing talismans:

- Water: Holding the talisman under running water or submerging it in a bowl of salt water is a simple and effective way to cleanse it. The water should be running or flowing to carry away any negative energies. After cleansing, be sure to dry the talisman thoroughly.

- Smoke: Burning sage, palo santo, or other cleansing herbs and passing the talisman through the smoke can cleanse it of any negative energies. The smoke should be allowed to completely surround the talisman.

- Sun or Moonlight: Placing the talisman in direct sunlight or moonlight can recharge and cleanse it. The light from the sun or moon should be allowed to completely envelop the talisman.

- Sound: Using a singing bowl, bell, or other musical instrument to create sound vibrations can cleanse the talisman. Simply hold the talisman in one hand and strike the instrument with the other, allowing the sound to wash over the talisman.

Before using the talisman for protection during a Ouija board session, it's important to cleanse it to remove any negative energies and vibrations it may have picked up. You can choose the method that resonates with you the most, or try different methods to find one that works best for you.

Set intentions:

Setting intentions is an important step to help focus your energy and direct the outcome of your Ouija board session. Here are some tips to help you set your intentions:

- Be specific: Your intentions should be specific and clear. Think about what you want to achieve or what you hope to gain from your Ouija board session. Maybe you want to connect with a specific loved one who has passed away or seek guidance on a particular issue. Whatever it is, be clear and specific in your intention.

- Use positive language: Your intentions should be stated in positive language. For example, instead of saying "I don't want to hear from any negative spirits," say "I only want to communicate with positive energies." This helps to focus your energy on what you want to achieve rather than what you want to avoid.

- Believe in your intentions: It's important to believe in your intentions and have faith that they will come to fruition. Your beliefs and energy play a crucial role in the success of your Ouija board session, so it's important to approach it with a positive and open mindset.

- Write down your intentions: Writing down your intentions can help to solidify them in your mind and serve as a reminder throughout the session. You can keep them nearby or even place them on the Ouija board itself.

By setting clear and positive intentions, you can focus your energy and direct the outcome of your Ouija board session towards your desired outcome. Remember to approach it with an open and positive mindset and trust in the process.

Wear or carry the talisman:

Wearing or carrying a talisman during your Ouija board session is a way to help protect yourself from negative energies and to bring positive energy into your space. Here are some tips on how to use a talisman:

- Choose a talisman that resonates with you: A talisman can be any object that holds meaning or significance to you, such as a piece of jewelry, a crystal, or a symbol. Choose a talisman that you feel drawn to or that has a special significance for you.

- Cleanse the talisman: Before using the talisman, it's important to cleanse it of any negative energy that may be attached to it. You can do this by holding it under running water, smudging it with sage or palo santo, or leaving it in the light of the full moon.

- Charge the talisman: Once the talisman is cleansed, you can charge it with your intention for the Ouija board session. Hold the talisman in your hands and focus your energy on it. Visualize positive energy flowing into the talisman and filling it with light.

- Wear or carry the talisman: During your Ouija board session, wear or carry the talisman with you to help protect yourself from negative energies and to bring positive energy into your space. You can also place the talisman on the Ouija board itself or in a prominent location in the room.

By wearing or carrying a talisman during your Ouija board session, you can help to protect yourself from negative energies and bring positive energy into your space. Remember to choose a talisman that resonates with you and to cleanse and charge it before using it.

Close the session properly:

Closing the session properly is an important step when using a Ouija board. It involves properly saying goodbye to any spirits or energies that may have been communicated with during the session. Failing to do so can leave the door open for negative energies or entities to linger.

One way to close the session is to thank the spirits or energies for communicating and express that the session is now ending. You can also ask for any energies or entities that were contacted during the session to leave and return to their own realm.

Some people also choose to cleanse the space again after the session has ended, using methods such as burning sage or lighting candles. This can help to further remove any residual negative energy.

It is important to avoid leaving the planchette on the board when the session is over, as this can also leave the door open for negative energy. Instead, properly store the board and planchette in a safe location until the next time they are needed.

It is also recommended to take a break between sessions, especially if there was any unsettling or negative energy present during the session. This allows time to clear and reset both the physical space and personal energy.

By using a protective talisman, you can create an extra layer of protection around yourself during a Ouija board session. Remember to choose a talisman that resonates with you and your intentions, and to set clear intentions for it to provide protection.

Never use the board alone:

Using a Ouija board alone is generally not recommended. It is always advisable to use the board with at least one other person. This is because having another person present can help to provide a sense of grounding and support during the session.

When using the board alone, it can be easier to become too immersed in the experience and lose touch with reality. This can lead to heightened anxiety or fear, as well as increased vulnerability to negative energies or entities.

Having a partner during the session can also provide a second perspective on any messages or communications received through the board. This can help to reduce the risk of misinterpretation or misunderstanding, which can sometimes occur when using the board alone.

In general, it is important to approach the use of the Ouija board with respect and caution, and to always prioritize safety and protection. This includes having at least one other person present during the session, as well as following all recommended precautions and guidelines.

Avoid negative emotions:

Negative emotions can create a powerful energy that can attract negative entities or spirits to the session. These entities can sometimes appear as threatening or hostile, causing fear and anxiety in those participating. Negative emotions can also cause those participating in the session to lose focus and become disoriented, leading to potentially harmful outcomes.
To avoid negative emotions during a session, it is important to take steps to create a positive and safe environment. This can be done by using the talisman, setting clear intentions, and calling upon positive energies or guides for protection.

Individuals should make sure that they are in a calm and centered state before beginning the session. This can be achieved through meditation or relaxation techniques.

If negative emotions do arise during the session, it is important to acknowledge them and release them before continuing. One way to do this is through deep breathing or visualization techniques, focusing on releasing the negative emotions and bringing in positive energies. Participants can also take a short break to regroup and ground themselves before continuing.

It is also important to avoid using the Ouija board while under the influence of drugs or alcohol. These substances can alter perception and judgment, making it difficult to remain focused and grounded during the session. This can increase the risk of negative experiences and potentially harmful outcomes.

By remaining calm, focused, and positive during the session, participants can create a safe and productive experience when using a Ouija board.

Don't invite the unknown:

When using a Ouija board, it is important to be cautious and mindful of the energies you are inviting into your space. One important rule to follow is to avoid inviting the unknown. This means that you should not attempt to contact spirits or entities that you know nothing about or have never encountered before.

Inviting the unknown can be dangerous because you cannot predict the nature of the energies that may respond to your invitation. There is no way of knowing if the spirit you are communicating with is benevolent or malevolent, and there is always the risk of attracting negative energies that could cause harm.

Another reason to avoid inviting the unknown is that it can attract unwanted attention to you and your space. By reaching out to spirits you know nothing about, you may inadvertently invite other entities to join the conversation. These additional spirits could have a negative influence on your session and potentially cause harm.

Furthermore, when you invite the unknown, you are opening yourself up to the possibility of encountering entities that may not have your best interests in mind. They may have their own agenda and may use the session to manipulate or deceive you.

When you invite the unknown, you may also attract lower level energies that have not yet evolved to a higher plane. These entities may be attracted to the energy of the board but may not have the ability to communicate effectively, which can lead to confusion and potentially dangerous situations.

It is also important to remember that spirits who are unfamiliar with you may not have your best interests in mind. They may not know how to communicate effectively or may not be aware of the harm they could be causing. Therefore, it is always best to be cautious and avoid inviting the unknown.

When using a Ouija board, it is important to only invite positive energies that you have a connection with. By avoiding the unknown, you can protect yourself and your space from unwanted energies that could cause harm or manipulate your session. Remember to always set clear intentions and use protective measures to ensure a safe and positive experience.

Set boundaries:

Setting boundaries is crucial when using a Ouija board. It is essential to have a clear understanding of what kind of communication is acceptable and what is not. It is also important to know how to end a session if things get out of hand.

Setting boundaries helps to maintain control and protect yourself and others from negative energy and harmful entities.

One way to set boundaries is by deciding what kind of questions or topics are off-limits during the session. This includes questions about death, the future, and personal information. It is also essential to decide what kind of entities you are willing to communicate with and what kind you are not. For example, you may want to communicate with benevolent spirits but not with malevolent ones.

Another way to set boundaries is by establishing a clear signal for ending the session. This can be a word, a gesture, or a specific action that indicates the session is over. It is important to communicate this signal to everyone involved in the session so that they know what to do if things get uncomfortable or dangerous.

It is important to limit the amount of time spent using the Ouija board. Long sessions can increase the risk of negative energy or harmful entities making contact. It is recommended to limit sessions to no more than 30 minutes at a time.

Another way to set boundaries is by using protective items such as crystals, amulets, or symbols. These can be used to create a protective barrier around the participants and the board. It is important to cleanse and charge these items regularly to ensure their effectiveness.

It is also important to set boundaries with other people who may be present during the session. This includes family members, friends, or other individuals who may be curious or skeptical. It is important to explain the risks involved in using the Ouija board and to ask for their respect and cooperation during the session.

Finally, it is important to trust your instincts and set boundaries that feel right for you. If at any point during the session you feel uncomfortable or unsafe, it is essential to end the session immediately. Remember, you are in control, and setting boundaries is an important part of maintaining that control.

By taking these precautions, you can help protect yourself from negative energies and entities and ensure a safe and positive experience with the Ouija board.

Chapter 3: The science behind the Ouija board

The Ouija board has been a source of fascination and controversy for decades, with some people believing that it is a tool for communicating with the spirit world, while others dismiss it as a mere toy. Despite the ongoing debate about its validity, the Ouija board has remained a popular and intriguing subject for scientists and researchers. In this chapter, we will explore the scientific theories and research behind the Ouija board.

While some people attribute the board's movement to the spirits, others believe that it is the result of the ideomotor effect, which is a psychological phenomenon where an individual's subconscious movements influence their physical actions. The ideomotor effect suggests that the participants are unwittingly moving the planchette themselves, rather than being guided by any external force.

There are studies that support the idea that the Ouija board works as a result of the ideomotor effect. For instance, a study conducted in the 1970s found that the board's movement could be attributed to the participants' unconscious movements. However, there is also research that suggests that the board's movement cannot be explained by the ideomotor effect alone, and that there may be other factors at play.

Another theory regarding the Ouija board's effectiveness is the concept of the "psychic telephone theory," which suggests that the board acts as a conduit for the subconscious mind to communicate with others. This theory proposes that the board's movements are not the result of any supernatural or spiritual force, but rather the result of the subconscious mind's ability to tap into universal consciousness and communicate through the board.

Some researchers have proposed that the Ouija board's effectiveness may be linked to quantum physics and the concept of non-locality. This theory suggests that the board is able to access information and energy from beyond the physical realm through quantum entanglement, which is the idea that particles can be connected regardless of their distance.

The science behind the Ouija board is a fascinating subject that continues to intrigue scientists and researchers. While some studies support the idea that the board's movement is the result of the ideomotor effect, others suggest that there may be more complex factors at play. In the following sections, we will delve deeper into each of these theories and explore the evidence supporting them.

Theories on how the Ouija board works

There are several theories about how the Ouija board works, and scientists have been studying this mysterious tool for decades. One of the most common theories is the ideomotor effect, which suggests that the movements of the planchette are caused by unconscious muscle movements, rather than any supernatural force. This means that the participants in the Ouija board session are unknowingly causing the planchette to move, often without realizing it.

Another theory is that the Ouija board works through the power of suggestion. This means that the participants are influenced by the expectations and beliefs of others in the group, which can lead to a kind of groupthink or shared consciousness. The subconscious minds of the participants may then create the illusion of a supernatural force guiding the planchette.

Some researchers have also suggested that the Ouija board may tap into the collective unconscious, a shared pool of knowledge and memories that exists within all humans. This theory suggests that the planchette movements may be guided by a kind of collective intelligence, rather than any individual consciousness.

Another theory is that the Ouija board is simply a tool for accessing the paranormal or spiritual realm. This theory suggests that the board is a conduit for communication with entities from beyond the physical world, such as spirits, ghosts, or demons.

Despite the many theories about how the Ouija board works, there is little scientific evidence to support any of them. The true nature of the Ouija board remains a mystery, and many people continue to use it as a tool for spiritual exploration or entertainment, while others believe it to be dangerous and avoid it altogether.

Scientific studies on the Ouija board

Scientific studies on the Ouija board have been conducted in attempts to explain its paranormal abilities. One such study was conducted by two neuroscientists, who found that the movements of the planchette on the Ouija board were the result of the ideomotor effect. The ideomotor effect is a phenomenon where the subconscious mind can influence the body to move involuntarily, without conscious awareness. In the case of the Ouija board, the subconscious mind of the participants may be directing the movements of the planchette, creating the illusion of communication with spirits.

Another study looked at the effects of the Ouija board on the brain using electroencephalography (EEG). The study found that when participants used the Ouija board, there was increased activity in the areas of the brain associated with self-referential thinking and semantic processing. This suggests that the use of the Ouija board may be a form of self-induced hypnosis, with the participants' subconscious minds guiding the movements of the planchette.

Despite these scientific explanations, there are still some unexplained phenomena associated with the Ouija board. For example, there are reports of the board spelling out messages that are highly specific and accurate, which some believe cannot be explained by the ideomotor effect alone. Additionally, there are many anecdotal accounts of the board moving without any apparent physical contact, which is difficult to explain using conventional scientific theories.

It's worth noting that some researchers have criticized the methodologies of these studies, arguing that they do not fully account for the complexities of the Ouija board experience. Furthermore, some believe that the Ouija board may tap into a realm of consciousness beyond the physical world, making it difficult to fully explain using conventional scientific methods.

While scientific studies have shed some light on the workings of the Ouija board, there is still much that remains mysterious and unexplained. Whether or not the board truly allows communication with spirits or is simply the result of subconscious movements, it remains a fascinating and often controversial tool for those interested in the paranormal.

Skeptical viewpoints on the Ouija board

Skeptical viewpoints on the Ouija board suggest that the movement of the planchette is due to the ideomotor effect. This effect occurs when a person's unconscious movements are guided by their thoughts or beliefs, without their conscious awareness. In the case of the Ouija board, skeptics argue that the movements of the planchette are influenced by the participants' subconscious thoughts and beliefs, rather than any external supernatural forces.

Skeptics also point out that the accuracy of the information provided by the Ouija board can be attributed to a phenomenon known as the "Barnum effect," which is the tendency for people to believe generic statements about themselves as being accurate and specifically tailored to them, even when they are not. This means that the vague and general messages received through the Ouija board may seem personally meaningful to the participants, even if they are not actually accurate or coming from a supernatural source.

Skeptics argue that the supposed supernatural powers of the Ouija board have never been scientifically proven, and that the experiences people have with the board can be explained by natural, psychological, and social factors.
They suggest that the Ouija board can be seen as a form of entertainment or a tool for exploring one's own subconscious, rather than a means of communicating with spirits or other supernatural entities.

Despite the skepticism surrounding the Ouija board, some researchers have attempted to study its effects in a scientific context. For example, a study published in the Journal of Nervous and Mental Disease in 2012 tested the effects of the Ouija board on participants' anxiety levels and found that it had no significant impact on anxiety. Another study published in the same journal in 2014 found that participants who believed in the paranormal were more likely to attribute meaning to the movements of the planchette than those who did not.

In conclusion, while the scientific evidence for the supernatural powers of the Ouija board is lacking, the board continues to fascinate and intrigue people around the world. Skeptics argue that the movements of the planchette are due to natural psychological and social factors, while believers maintain that the board can communicate with the spirit world. Regardless of one's perspective, the Ouija board remains a unique cultural artifact with a rich history and ongoing controversy.

Chapter 4: Real-life experiences with the Ouija board

The Ouija board has been a popular tool for communicating with the spiritual realm for over a century, and as such, there have been many stories and experiences associated with its use. Some people have had positive experiences that have helped them connect with loved ones who have passed on, while others have had negative experiences that have left them feeling scared and traumatized. In this chapter, we will explore some of these real-life experiences, both positive and negative, and try to understand what may have caused them.

True stories of people's experiences with the Ouija board

Many people who have used the Ouija board report feeling an intense and palpable energy during their sessions. Some describe feeling a cold breeze or seeing objects move around the room. Others claim to have seen apparitions or experienced unexplainable phenomena.

One common theme among many Ouija board users is the experience of receiving messages from deceased loved ones. People report feeling a strong connection to their departed family members or friends and receiving messages that they feel could not have come from anyone else.

Some users have reported feeling a strong presence or energy that they believe to be demonic or negative in nature. These experiences can be very frightening and can leave lasting psychological effects on the user.

Other users have reported feeling a sense of peace or enlightenment during their Ouija board sessions. They describe feeling a connection to a higher power or spiritual energy that helps them to better understand their place in the world.

In some cases, people have reported experiencing physical symptoms during or after using the Ouija board. These symptoms can range from mild headaches or nausea to more serious issues like seizures or fainting spells.

There have been reports of people becoming obsessed with using the Ouija board and spending countless hours communicating with spirits. Some have even claimed that the board has become an addiction for them, causing them to neglect other aspects of their lives.

While many people believe that the Ouija board can be a tool for communicating with spirits, others view it as a purely psychological phenomenon. These skeptics argue that the movements of the planchette are caused by the users' unconscious movements and that any messages received are simply a reflection of the users' own thoughts and desires.

Some people believe that the Ouija board can be a dangerous tool that should not be used without proper training or guidance. They argue that the board can be used by malevolent spirits to gain access to the physical world and cause harm to the users.

There have been numerous accounts of people experiencing negative consequences after using the Ouija board, including physical harm, emotional distress, and even possession. These experiences have led some to believe that the board is a gateway to the spirit world that should not be opened lightly.

Despite the controversy surrounding the Ouija board, it remains a popular tool for those seeking to communicate with spirits. Many people believe that the board can offer a unique and powerful experience, allowing them to connect with loved ones who have passed on or gain a deeper understanding of the spiritual realm.

As with any tool or practice, it is important to approach the Ouija board with caution and respect. Users should be aware of the potential risks and take steps to protect themselves from negative energy or unwanted spirits.

Whether you believe in the spiritual power of the Ouija board or not, it is clear that the tool has had a profound impact on countless people's lives. Its ability to connect people with the unseen world has fascinated and intrigued people for generations, and its legacy is sure to continue for many years to come.

The dangers of using the Ouija board

there are many potential dangers associated with using the Ouija board, both physical and psychological. Some of the physical dangers include accidentally burning oneself with candles or incense, or even tripping and falling in the dark if proper lighting is not used. However, the more serious dangers are often psychological or spiritual in nature.

One of the main dangers of using the Ouija board is that it can attract negative or malevolent entities. Some people believe that these entities are attracted to the board itself, while others believe that they are attracted to the energy that is generated during a session. Regardless of the reason, it is important to remember that not all spirits are benevolent and some may have ill intentions towards those using the board.

Another danger is the potential for the board to become a gateway or portal for negative entities to enter into our world. Some people believe that using the Ouija board can open up a doorway between the physical realm and the spiritual realm, and that this doorway can allow entities to cross over. This can be especially dangerous if the entity that comes through is malevolent or harmful in some way.

Furthermore, the Ouija board can also be a source of psychological harm. It is not uncommon for people to become obsessed with the board and the messages that it produces. This can lead to an unhealthy preoccupation with the board and the spirit world, which can cause anxiety, depression, and other psychological issues.

Using the Ouija board can sometimes lead to the development of psychic abilities, which can be both a gift and a curse. While some people may find these abilities to be empowering and helpful, others may find them overwhelming or even frightening.

Using the Ouija board can also lead to a loss of personal power and control. Some people report feeling as though they are being controlled or manipulated by the spirits they are communicating with, and this loss of control can be very unsettling.

Another danger of using the Ouija board is that it can attract the attention of negative entities that can attach themselves to the user. These entities can cause a range of physical, emotional, and psychological symptoms, including depression, anxiety, fatigue, and even physical illness.

Using the Ouija board can be addictive, and some people may find it difficult to stop using it once they have started. This addiction can be fueled by the sense of power and connection that comes from communicating with spirits, but it can also be fueled by a desire for validation or attention.

Furthermore, using the Ouija board can also lead to the manipulation or deception of the users. Some entities may pretend to be someone or something they are not, and this can lead to confusion, frustration, and even harm.

Another danger of using the Ouija board is that it can cause rifts in relationships, especially if one person involved in the session is more skeptical or uncomfortable with the process than the others. This can lead to feelings of mistrust, resentment, and even outright conflict.

While the Ouija board can be a fascinating and intriguing tool for exploring the spirit world, it is important to approach it with caution and respect. The potential dangers associated with its use are very real, and it is important to be aware of them before attempting to communicate with the unknown. By taking appropriate precautions and using the board responsibly, however, it is possible to have a safe and positive experience with this enigmatic tool.

The potential consequences of using the Ouija board

While the use of the Ouija board can be intriguing and even thrilling to some, it is important to be aware of the potential consequences and dangers involved. Here are some potential consequences that may result from using the Ouija board:

Inviting negative energies:

Inviting negative energies is one of the most significant dangers of using the Ouija board. When using the board, you are opening up a portal to the spirit world, and you never know what kind of energy may come through. Negative energies can attach themselves to individuals or follow them home, causing distress, illness, and even possession. These energies can be dangerous and difficult to remove without professional help.

Another potential consequence of inviting negative energies is the manifestation of negative events in one's life. When individuals intentionally or unintentionally invite negative energy, it can have a ripple effect on their lives. They may experience a series of unfortunate events, such as accidents, illnesses, and financial problems. Negative energies can also lead to a decrease in mental and emotional health, including depression, anxiety, and paranoia.

Another danger of using the Ouija board is the potential for deception. Negative energies may disguise themselves as positive spirits or loved ones, leading individuals to believe they are receiving guidance or messages from a trusted source. However, these energies may have ulterior motives and use deception to gain control over an individual's thoughts, emotions, and actions.

The Ouija board can attract and amplify negative energy already present in a space. If the board is used in an area with a history of negative events or emotions, it can intensify these energies and make them more difficult to dispel.

One potential consequence of using the Ouija board is the psychological impact it can have on individuals. It can lead to a loss of sense of control, as individuals may feel that they are not in control of their thoughts or actions. Additionally, it can cause feelings of guilt, shame, and anxiety, as individuals may feel that they have opened themselves up to negative energy and put themselves in danger.

Another potential danger of using the Ouija board is the possibility of creating negative thought forms or entities. These are created by negative energy and can linger long after the board has been put away. Negative thought forms can lead to disturbances in the environment and the creation of negative energy that can affect individuals in the surrounding area.

Using the Ouija board can lead to an addiction to the board and the act of communicating with the spirit world. This addiction can be harmful, leading to a loss of control over one's life and an obsession with the board. It can lead to negative impacts on mental, physical, and emotional health and disrupt relationships and daily life.

Using the Ouija board can be a dangerous and potentially harmful activity. It is important to be aware of the potential consequences and dangers before using the board and to take precautions to protect oneself and others.

Psychic attacks:

Psychic attacks are another potential danger of using the Ouija board. Psychic attacks are instances where a person or entity deliberately targets and harms another person using their own energy or psychic abilities. When using the Ouija board, individuals may unknowingly invite negative or malevolent entities to communicate with them. These entities may try to manipulate the user or even attack them psychically.

Psychic attacks can have a wide range of effects on the victim, including physical and emotional symptoms. Some common physical symptoms of a psychic attack include headaches, fatigue, and body aches. Emotional symptoms may include anxiety, depression, and feelings of paranoia. In severe cases, a psychic attack may even lead to possession by a negative entity.

It is important to note that not everyone believes in psychic attacks, and some skeptics may dismiss them as purely psychological phenomena. However, those who have experienced such attacks may attest to their reality and the potential dangers of using the Ouija board.

To protect oneself from psychic attacks when using the Ouija board, it is important to set strong intentions and boundaries before beginning the session. It is also recommended to call on protective energies or entities, such as angels or spirit guides, to assist in keeping the session safe. Additionally, wearing or carrying a protective talisman, such as a crystal or piece of jewelry, may provide added protection.

The potential for psychic attacks when using the Ouija board highlights the importance of approaching its use with caution and respect. It is crucial to always prioritize personal safety and well-being when engaging in any spiritual or paranormal practices.

Attachment of negative entities:

Another potential danger of using the Ouija board is the attachment of negative entities. When you open yourself up to communication with the spirit world, you may inadvertently attract negative energies that can attach themselves to you or the space in which you are using the board. These entities may be angry, malicious, or seeking to cause harm, and they may not leave easily.

Once an entity has attached itself, it can cause a range of negative effects, including physical illness, emotional distress, and psychological disorders. Some people have reported experiencing sudden changes in behavior or personality, such as becoming aggressive or withdrawn. Others have reported feeling constantly drained of energy or experiencing unexplained mood swings.

Removing a negative entity can be a difficult and lengthy process, often requiring the help of a professional such as a psychic, shaman, or energy healer. It is important to take precautions to avoid attracting negative energies in the first place and to seek help if you suspect that you or someone else has been affected.

It is also important to note that the attachment of negative entities is not limited to the use of the Ouija board. Any type of spiritual communication or interaction with the spirit world carries a potential risk of attracting negative energies. However, the Ouija board is often seen as a particularly risky tool because it allows for direct and unfiltered communication with spirits, without the protection of a trained practitioner or medium.

It is important to be aware of the potential dangers of using the Ouija board and to approach it with caution and respect. If you choose to use the board, it is recommended that you do so with a clear intention, a strong sense of protection, and in the presence of a trained practitioner or medium. If you experience any negative effects, seek help immediately.

False or misleading information:

Another danger of using the Ouija board is the possibility of receiving false or misleading information. Since the board works through the participants' subconscious minds, it's possible for them to receive messages that are not accurate or reliable. The messages may also be influenced by the participants' expectations, beliefs, and biases, which can further distort the accuracy of the information received.

In some cases, the participants may intentionally manipulate the board to receive false or misleading information. This can be done for various reasons, such as to prank others, to prove a point, or to gain attention. However, such actions can have serious consequences, as the recipients of the false information may act upon it and make decisions based on it.

Furthermore, it's important to note that the Ouija board is not a reliable tool for divination or spiritual guidance. Its accuracy and effectiveness have not been scientifically proven, and it should not be used as a substitute for professional advice or therapy. Relying too heavily on the board for important decisions or life choices can lead to negative consequences and regret.

The Ouija board can be a dangerous tool that should be approached with caution and respect. The potential consequences of using the board include inviting negative energies, psychic attacks, attachment of negative entities, and receiving false or misleading information. It's important to be aware of these risks and to take measures to protect oneself before and after using the board. Ultimately, the best course of action may be to avoid using the Ouija board altogether and to seek guidance and advice from more reliable sources.

Increased susceptibility to negative influences:

Another potential danger of using the Ouija board is the increased susceptibility to negative influences. When individuals engage in Ouija board sessions, they may become more open to negative energies and influences. This can lead to a number of negative consequences, including increased anxiety, depression, and mood swings.

The use of the Ouija board can also lead to an increase in addictive behavior, as individuals may become addicted to the feeling of power or control that comes from using the board. This addiction can then lead to an increased vulnerability to negative influences and behaviors.

The Ouija board can also serve as a gateway to other negative or dangerous spiritual practices, such as black magic or other forms of witchcraft. This can lead individuals down a dangerous and potentially destructive path, causing them to engage in harmful or illegal activities.

There is also the potential for psychological harm when using the Ouija board. For example, individuals may experience confusion, disorientation, or even psychosis as a result of using the board. This can be particularly dangerous for those with pre-existing mental health conditions, as it can exacerbate their symptoms and lead to further distress.

Using the Ouija board can also lead to spiritual and emotional turmoil. Individuals may experience feelings of guilt, shame, or fear as a result of using the board, particularly if they believe they have contacted negative entities or spirits. This can lead to feelings of isolation or alienation, as individuals may feel that they cannot confide in others about their experiences.

The dangers of using the Ouija board should not be taken lightly. While some individuals may have positive experiences using the board, the potential for negative consequences is significant. As such, it is important to carefully consider the potential risks before deciding to use the board, and to take appropriate precautions to ensure that you are protected from harm.

Interference with personal beliefs or religious practices:

Another potential danger of using the Ouija board is the interference it can have with personal beliefs or religious practices. Some individuals may feel that using the board goes against their religious beliefs or personal values. For example, some religious groups believe that the Ouija board is a tool of the devil or is used to communicate with malevolent spirits.

Using the board may also conflict with personal beliefs about death and the afterlife. The idea of communicating with the dead through a board may be unsettling or even offensive to some individuals. Additionally, the board's messages may conflict with the individual's beliefs about the nature of the afterlife, causing confusion or distress.

The Ouija board can potentially lead to a loss of faith in one's personal beliefs or religious practices. If an individual receives messages through the board that contradict their beliefs or experiences, they may begin to question their faith and struggle with doubt and uncertainty.

It is important to note that the potential interference with personal beliefs or religious practices is not limited to those who actively use the Ouija board. Simply being exposed to the board and its messages through media or social circles can also have an impact on an individual's beliefs and values.

The potential interference with personal beliefs or religious practices highlights the importance of considering one's values and beliefs before engaging with the Ouija board. It is essential to approach the board with an open mind, but also to maintain a strong sense of self and personal values.

Difficulty disconnecting:

Another potential danger of using the Ouija board is the difficulty in disconnecting from the session. Even if the participants close the session properly, there is a chance that they may still feel a lingering presence or energy around them. This can result in feelings of anxiety, unease, and even paranoia. In some cases, people have reported experiencing nightmares, hallucinations, and other disturbing phenomena long after using the Ouija board.

Some people may become addicted to using the Ouija board, seeking out more and more sessions in an attempt to connect with the other side. This can lead to a dangerous obsession with the paranormal, and can interfere with their ability to function in daily life. Some people may even begin to neglect their responsibilities and relationships in order to continue using the board.

Another potential consequence of using the Ouija board is that it can cause rifts in relationships between the participants.

This can happen if one person becomes convinced that the board is providing accurate information, while another person remains skeptical. Disagreements can arise over whether the information provided by the board is real or imagined, and this can create tension and mistrust between friends or family members.

It is important to note that many religious and cultural traditions consider the use of the Ouija board to be taboo or even sinful. For example, some Christians believe that the board is a tool of the devil and that using it can invite demonic influence into one's life. Similarly, many Indigenous cultures believe that communicating with the dead in this way is disrespectful and can anger the spirits. If a person's personal beliefs or practices are in conflict with the use of the Ouija board, they may experience feelings of guilt or shame after using it.

While the Ouija board can be a fascinating and intriguing tool for communicating with the paranormal, it is important to be aware of the potential dangers and consequences of using it. These can include inviting negative energies, psychic attacks, attachment of negative entities, false or misleading information, increased susceptibility to negative influences, interference with personal beliefs or religious practices, difficulty disconnecting, and even rifts in relationships. Before deciding to use the board, it is important to consider these risks and to proceed with caution.

Increased fear or anxiety:

When people use the Ouija board, they are opening themselves up to the unknown and the paranormal. This can cause fear and anxiety, especially if the experience is negative. Many people report feeling a sense of unease or discomfort during and after using the board, and these feelings can linger for a long time.

Using the Ouija board can even trigger or worsen anxiety disorders, such as panic attacks or generalized anxiety disorder. This is because the experience of communicating with spirits or entities beyond our physical reality can be overwhelming and unsettling for some individuals.

The fear and anxiety associated with the Ouija board can spill over into other areas of a person's life. For example, they may become more fearful or paranoid in general, or they may become more anxious about death and the afterlife.

It is important to note that these potential consequences are not experienced by everyone who uses the Ouija board. However, it is important to be aware of the risks and to approach the board with caution and respect. It is also important to listen to your instincts and stop using the board if you feel uncomfortable or unsafe in any way.

In order to minimize the risk of increased fear or anxiety, it is important to set boundaries and to take breaks between sessions. It is also helpful to have a support system of friends or loved ones who can provide comfort and reassurance.

While the Ouija board can be a fascinating tool for exploring the paranormal, it is not without its risks.
Increased fear or anxiety is one potential consequence of using the board, and it is important to approach the experience with caution and respect. By setting boundaries, taking breaks, and seeking support, individuals can minimize the risk of negative consequences and have a more positive experience with the board.

Physical harm:

While it is rare, there have been reports of physical harm resulting from the use of the Ouija board. Some individuals have reported feeling physically drained or experiencing unexplained bruises or scratches after using the board. There have also been cases where individuals have claimed to have been pushed or attacked by unseen forces while using the board.

One potential explanation for this physical harm is the idea of psychokinetic energy. This is the theory that the human mind has the ability to influence physical objects and events through the power of thought. It is possible that the intense focus and emotional energy that is often involved in using the Ouija board could lead to the unintentional release of psychokinetic energy, which could manifest in physical ways.

Another possibility is that negative entities or spirits may be attracted to the energy that is created during Ouija board sessions, and may seek to harm or possess those who are using the board. While this is a controversial idea, many people who have had negative experiences with the Ouija board believe that they were targeted by malevolent entities.

It is important to note that the potential for physical harm is not the only danger associated with the Ouija board, and it is not the most common. However, it is important to be aware of this risk and to approach the use of the board with caution and respect.

Addiction or obsession:

Another potential danger of using the Ouija board is the risk of addiction or obsession. For some individuals, the experience of using the Ouija board can be thrilling and exhilarating, leading them to become addicted to the practice. This addiction can lead to an obsession with communicating with the spirits and can ultimately consume the individual's life.

Those who become addicted to using the Ouija board may find that they cannot function normally without it. They may spend all their free time using the board or seeking out new opportunities to communicate with spirits. This can lead to neglecting important responsibilities, such as work, school, and relationships.

Addiction to using the Ouija board can also lead to financial strain, as individuals may spend money on expensive Ouija board sets or psychic readings to enhance their experience. In some cases, individuals may also seek out the services of a professional medium or psychic, which can be costly.

Addiction to using the Ouija board can also have negative effects on mental health. The constant pursuit of communication with spirits can lead to heightened levels of anxiety, stress, and paranoia. This can ultimately lead to mental health issues such as depression and anxiety disorders.

It is important to note that addiction or obsession with the Ouija board is not common and usually only occurs in a small minority of individuals. However, it is still a potential danger that should not be overlooked.

While the use of the Ouija board may seem harmless and fun, it can also come with a variety of potential dangers and risks. It is important to approach the practice with caution and respect, and to be aware of the potential consequences that may arise.

Strain on relationships:

Using the Ouija board can also lead to a strain on relationships. People who become obsessed with using the board may neglect their personal and professional responsibilities, causing conflicts with family members, friends, and colleagues. Loved ones may become concerned about the individual's behavior and well-being, which can lead to tension and strain on the relationship. Additionally, if one person in a relationship is uncomfortable with the idea of using the Ouija board and the other is insistent on using it, this can create tension and conflict.

If a negative entity is believed to have attached itself to someone who has used the Ouija board, this can create tension and strain on relationships. The person may begin to exhibit erratic or hostile behavior, which can be frightening for those around them. This can lead to the breakdown of relationships and social isolation for the person experiencing the negative effects of the Ouija board.

In some cases, using the Ouija board may lead to the development of new relationships, such as with spirits or entities believed to be contacted through the board. These relationships can become obsessive, with individuals spending increasing amounts of time communicating with these entities to the detriment of their personal relationships.

It's also possible for the use of the Ouija board to create tension and conflict within religious communities. Some religious groups view the board as a tool for communicating with demons or other negative entities, and using it may be seen as a violation of religious beliefs or practices. This can lead to conflict with others in the religious community, causing strain on those relationships.

The use of the Ouija board can lead to mistrust or even betrayal within relationships. People may feel deceived or betrayed by others who have convinced them to use the board or who have misled them about its potential consequences. This can create feelings of anger, resentment, and distrust that can be difficult to overcome.

Negative influence on mental health:

One of the most significant dangers of using the Ouija board is the potential negative impact it can have on one's mental health. Many people who use the board report experiencing intense fear, anxiety, and even paranoia during and after their sessions. This can be particularly true for individuals who are already struggling with mental health issues such as depression or anxiety.

Some people who use the Ouija board may become obsessed with it, leading to a compulsion to use it regularly. This can interfere with their daily lives and cause significant distress. In some cases, this obsession can lead to addiction, which can be challenging to overcome.

The Ouija board may also lead to an increased risk of developing mental health issues such as dissociative identity disorder (DID) or psychosis. These conditions involve a detachment from reality and can be triggered or exacerbated by experiences such as using the board. It is essential to note that while these conditions are relatively rare, they are serious and can have a significant impact on one's life.

Furthermore, using the Ouija board can also lead to sleep disturbances, such as nightmares and insomnia. The intense emotions and thoughts that can arise during a session can carry over into sleep and impact the quality of rest one gets. Over time, this can lead to chronic sleep deprivation, which can contribute to a range of physical and mental health problems.

The Ouija board's potential negative influence on mental health can strain relationships with loved ones. Friends and family members may not understand the appeal of using the board and may be concerned about the impact it is having on the user's well-being. This can lead to conflict and tension, which can be challenging to navigate and resolve.

While using the Ouija board may seem like harmless fun, it is essential to consider the potential consequences carefully. The negative impact it can have on one's mental health is not to be taken lightly, and users should approach the board with caution and respect. If one is struggling with mental health issues, it is recommended to avoid using the board altogether.

It is important to weigh these potential consequences carefully before deciding whether or not to use the Ouija board. If you do choose to use it, taking proper precautions and being aware of the potential dangers can help mitigate these risks.

Chapter 5: The spiritual and religious aspects of the Ouija board

The Ouija board has been a topic of interest and concern for various religious groups and spiritual beliefs, with some viewing it as a tool of communication with the spirit world and others condemning it as a tool of the devil. The board's ability to communicate with the unknown has been a source of fascination for those who believe in the existence of spirits and the afterlife, as well as those who are curious about the unknown. This chapter explores the various religious and spiritual beliefs surrounding the Ouija board and how they have shaped perceptions of its use.

Different cultural beliefs and practices surrounding the Ouija board

The Ouija board has been a part of spiritual and religious practices across various cultures and belief systems for centuries. Different cultural beliefs and practices surrounding the Ouija board often vary widely, with some viewing it as a harmless tool for communication with spirits and others viewing it as a tool for demonic possession and spiritual harm.

In some African cultures, the Ouija board is viewed as a powerful tool for communicating with ancestors and spirits. In Haiti, for example, the Ouija board is often used in Voodoo ceremonies as a way of contacting the dead. Similarly, in certain Native American cultures, the Ouija board is used for divination and communication with spirits.

In some Eastern cultures, the Ouija board is viewed as a tool for spiritual growth and self-discovery. In Japan, for example, the Ouija board is often used as a form of meditation and self-reflection. In China, the Ouija board is used in Taoist practices as a way of communicating with spirits and gaining spiritual insights.

In Western culture, the Ouija board has been associated with both spiritualism and occult practices. In the late 19th and early 20th centuries, the Ouija board was popularized as a tool for communicating with the dead during the Spiritualist movement. However, with the rise of the occult and New Age movements, the Ouija board has become associated with darker spiritual practices and the potential for demonic possession.

Some Christian groups view the Ouija board as a tool of the devil and actively discourage its use. Other religious groups, such as Wiccans and Pagans, may use the Ouija board as part of their spiritual practices.

Despite the variations in cultural beliefs and practices surrounding the Ouija board, one common thread is the belief that it is a powerful tool for communicating with spirits and the supernatural realm. Whether viewed as a harmless form of divination or a tool for demonic possession, the Ouija board continues to hold a place in spiritual and religious practices across the world.

The Ouija board's connection to the supernatural and the paranormal

The Ouija board is often associated with the supernatural and paranormal due to its supposed ability to communicate with entities beyond the physical realm. Some people believe that the board is a portal to the spirit world and that it allows spirits or other entities to communicate with the living. This connection to the supernatural and paranormal has been a subject of interest for many people, including paranormal investigators, spiritualists, and those interested in the occult.

Many cultures around the world have their own beliefs about the afterlife and the existence of spirits. In some cultures, the belief in spirits is deeply ingrained in daily life, and the use of tools like the Ouija board is seen as a way to connect with the spirit world. However, other cultures view the Ouija board with suspicion and even fear, as it is seen as a tool that can attract malevolent spirits or demons.

Some people who have used the Ouija board have reported experiencing supernatural or paranormal phenomena, such as objects moving on their own, strange sounds or voices, and even sightings of apparitions or ghosts. These experiences have led some to believe that the board is truly capable of communicating with the other side. However, others remain skeptical and attribute these experiences to psychological or natural causes.

The connection between the Ouija board and the supernatural has also been explored in popular culture, including films, television shows, and books. The board has been featured in horror movies and other works of fiction that explore the paranormal or supernatural, often portraying it as a tool that can unleash dark and dangerous forces.

Despite its association with the supernatural and paranormal, the Ouija board remains a controversial and often misunderstood tool. While some believe that it can provide a genuine connection to the spirit world, others view it as a mere game or hoax. The debate continues among believers and skeptics alike, with no clear consensus on the true nature of the board's connection to the supernatural.

Religious opinions and criticisms of the Ouija board

Religious opinions and criticisms of the Ouija board vary widely across different faiths and denominations. Many religions view the use of Ouija boards as dangerous and forbidden, while others believe it to be a tool for communicating with the dead or other entities. Here are some examples of different religious views on the Ouija board:

Christianity:

In Christianity, the use of the Ouija board is generally discouraged, if not outright condemned, due to its connection to the occult and potential for negative spiritual influence. Many Christians believe that the board is a tool of Satan or other malevolent entities, and that using it opens the user up to demonic possession or oppression.

Some Christian groups go as far as to say that the Ouija board is a form of divination, which is explicitly prohibited in the Bible. The book of Deuteronomy, for example, warns against seeking knowledge from the dead or other spiritual sources outside of God, stating that such practices are an abomination.

Moreover, some Christian authorities claim that the Ouija board can have a harmful effect on the soul, leading individuals down a path of spiritual destruction. It is also said to go against the fundamental principle of faith, which requires individuals to trust in God's plan for their lives rather than seeking guidance from other sources.

However, not all Christians share this view, and there are many who believe that the Ouija board is simply a harmless game or tool for communication with spirits. Some even argue that it can be used for good, such as in the case of seeking guidance from deceased loved ones or helping to solve mysteries.

Regardless of individual beliefs, it is important to note that the use of the Ouija board is a personal decision and should be approached with caution and respect for one's own spiritual beliefs and practices.

Islam:

In Islam, the use of the Ouija board is considered haram or forbidden as it is believed to be a form of divination and seeking knowledge of the unseen, which is strictly prohibited.
Islam also teaches that communication with the dead is not possible, and any attempt to do so is considered an act of disbelief. Therefore, using the Ouija board to communicate with spirits or deceased loved ones is viewed as a violation of Islamic beliefs.

In some Muslim countries, the possession and sale of the Ouija board is illegal, and those caught using it may face punishment. Some Islamic scholars warn against the dangers of using the Ouija board, stating that it can lead to possession by evil spirits, psychological disorders, and even death.

Some Muslims may still use the Ouija board, especially those who are not strictly adherent to Islamic teachings. In these cases, it is often viewed as a form of entertainment rather than a serious spiritual practice.

The Islamic stance on the Ouija board is one of strong condemnation and prohibition, with a belief that it goes against the fundamental teachings of the religion.

Judaism:

In Judaism, the use of the Ouija board is generally discouraged, if not outright prohibited, as it is considered to be a form of divination, which is viewed as a violation of the Jewish prohibition against consulting with mediums or necromancers (Deuteronomy 18:10-12). According to Jewish belief, only God has the power to communicate with the dead, and attempting to do so through the Ouija board or other means is seen as a challenge to God's authority.

In Jewish tradition, the dead are not to be disturbed or communicated with, as doing so can lead to negative consequences. The practice of communicating with the dead is viewed as dangerous and potentially opening oneself up to malevolent spiritual forces. Additionally, the use of the Ouija board may be seen as a form of idolatry, as it involves seeking guidance or information from sources other than God.

While there may be some Jewish individuals or groups who do use the Ouija board, it is generally not accepted within the larger Jewish community. Rabbis and other religious leaders may strongly discourage or prohibit its use, particularly among young people who may be more susceptible to its allure. In summary, within the Jewish faith, the use of the Ouija board is generally discouraged or prohibited due to its association with divination, which is considered a violation of Jewish law, as well as its potential to disturb the dead and open oneself up to negative spiritual forces.

Hinduism:

Hinduism is a diverse religion with many different beliefs and practices, and as such, there is no single unified view on the Ouija board. However, some Hindus believe that using the Ouija board can be a dangerous practice that can attract negative energies and entities. They believe that these negative energies and entities can cause harm to those who use the board and can also cause disruptions to their spiritual practices.

Others view the Ouija board as a tool that can be used to connect with spiritual energies and entities in a positive and constructive way. They believe that the board can be used to communicate with loved ones who have passed on or with spiritual guides and mentors who can offer guidance and wisdom.

In Hinduism, there is also a belief in the importance of maintaining a balance between the physical and spiritual worlds. Some believe that using the Ouija board can disrupt this balance and cause negative consequences. Others believe that the board can be used as a tool to strengthen this balance and help individuals connect more deeply with the spiritual world.

While there is no single view on the Ouija board in Hinduism, it is generally believed that using the board requires caution, respect, and an understanding of the potential risks and benefits involved.

Native American Spirituality:

Native American spirituality varies among tribes, but many have their own beliefs and practices regarding the spirit world and communication with the dead. Some tribes view the Ouija board as a tool of the devil or a portal for malevolent spirits, while others view it as a harmless game.

One of the main concerns for Native Americans regarding the Ouija board is the potential for cultural appropriation. Some individuals and companies have marketed "Native American Ouija boards," which have been criticized as disrespectful and exploitative of indigenous cultures.

Some Native American tribes have their own traditions of communicating with spirits, such as through dream visions or the use of sacred herbs. The use of the Ouija board may be seen as a disrespectful or inappropriate alternative to these traditional practices.

Native American views on the Ouija board are diverse and often tied to individual tribal beliefs and practices. However, many tribal members may caution against its use and emphasize the importance of respecting indigenous cultures and traditions.

Wicca and Paganism:

Wicca and Paganism are modern spiritual movements that are often associated with the use of the Ouija board. These belief systems view the board as a tool for communication with the spirit world and often incorporate it into their practices.

In Wicca, the Ouija board is often used during divination rituals, where it is believed to facilitate communication with the dead or other spiritual entities. However, some Wiccans warn against the use of the board, cautioning that it can be dangerous and should only be used by experienced practitioners.

In Paganism, the Ouija board is often used as a means of contacting the dead or other spirits. Some Pagans believe that the board can be used to gain knowledge or guidance from spiritual entities, while others caution that it can attract negative energies and should be used with caution.
Overall, both Wicca and Paganism view the Ouija board as a tool for spiritual communication and exploration. However, there are differing opinions on its use

and potential dangers, with some practitioners embracing it and others warning against its use without proper training and experience.

The use of the Ouija board has been a controversial topic in many religious circles, with differing opinions on whether it is a tool for communication with the supernatural or a dangerous and forbidden practice.

Chapter 6: The psychology of the Ouija board

The Ouija board is a unique tool that has been utilized for centuries, with people seeking to communicate with the unknown or the spirit realm. While some people approach it as a game or a form of entertainment, others believe in its ability to connect with the supernatural. Despite the divided beliefs surrounding the Ouija board, there is no doubt that its use has psychological implications. In this chapter, we will explore the psychological aspects of the Ouija board and how it can affect the human mind. We will look into the theories and ideas of psychologists regarding the use of the Ouija board, including the ideomotor effect, cognitive dissonance, and more. We will also explore the reasons why people are drawn to the Ouija board, the potential risks involved, and the impact it can have on mental health. Finally, we will examine the ethical concerns surrounding its use and whether or not the Ouija board should be considered a legitimate tool for psychological therapy.

The psychological effects of using the Ouija board

here are some points on the psychological effects of using the Ouija board:

Priming:

priming is a psychological concept that refers to the unconscious influence of stimuli on a person's subsequent behavior or responses. It can occur when an initial stimulus or cue unconsciously influences a person's perception, behavior, or response to a subsequent stimulus or situation. In the context of the Ouija board, priming could occur when a person's preconceived beliefs or expectations about the board and its abilities influence their responses or movements of the planchette.

For example, if a person believes that the Ouija board can communicate with spirits, they may unconsciously move the planchette in a way that supports this belief, even if they are not aware of doing so. Alternatively, if a person believes that the Ouija board is just a game, they may not take it seriously and may not be influenced by it in the same way.

The influence of priming can be especially strong when a person is in an altered state of consciousness or under the influence of drugs or alcohol. In such situations, a person may be more susceptible to external cues and less able to exert conscious control over their behavior and responses.

It is worth noting that while priming may play a role in the use of the Ouija board, it does not necessarily explain all of the board's phenomena. Other psychological and paranormal factors may also be involved.

Ideomotor effect:

The ideomotor effect is a psychological phenomenon that can help explain how the Ouija board works. It is the unconscious, involuntary movement of our muscles in response to an idea or suggestion. In other words, our thoughts and beliefs can influence our physical actions without us being consciously aware of it.

The ideomotor effect has been studied extensively in psychology and is a well-established phenomenon. It can occur in many different contexts, such as during hypnosis, meditation, and even in everyday activities like driving or typing on a keyboard. It is thought to be a natural part of the way our brains process information and coordinate our movements.

When it comes to the Ouija board, the ideomotor effect is believed to be the explanation for the movement of the planchette. Participants may think that they are not moving the planchette themselves, but in fact, their unconscious movements are directing it. This can create the illusion that some external force is controlling the board, leading people to believe that they are communicating with spirits or other supernatural entities.

There have been numerous studies on the ideomotor effect and the Ouija board. In one study, participants were blindfolded and told that the board was upside down. Despite this, the planchette still moved and participants reported receiving messages from the board. This suggests that the movement of the planchette is not due to any external force, but rather to the participants' own unconscious movements.

While the ideomotor effect may seem like a simple explanation for the Ouija board, it is important to consider its implications. It suggests that our beliefs and expectations can have a powerful influence on our perceptions and behaviors, even when we are not consciously aware of it. This means that the Ouija board can be a powerful tool for exploring our own thoughts and beliefs, but it also highlights the importance of approaching it with caution and skepticism.

Confirmation bias:

Confirmation bias is another psychological factor that can play a role in the use of Ouija boards. It is a tendency for people to interpret information in a way that confirms their preexisting beliefs or expectations. In the context of Ouija boards, confirmation bias can lead people to interpret ambiguous or random movements of the planchette as deliberate messages from spirits or entities, even if there is no evidence to support such a belief.

For example, if a person using a Ouija board believes in the existence of a specific spirit or entity, they may unconsciously seek out messages or movements that seem to support their belief, while ignoring or dismissing those that do not. This can result in a feedback loop where the person's belief in the spirit or entity is reinforced by their interpretation of the Ouija board's movements, leading to a stronger belief and a greater willingness to use the board in the future.

Confirmation bias can also be influenced by the social dynamics of a Ouija board session. If several people are using the board together, they may unconsciously or consciously influence each other's beliefs and interpretations of the board's movements. This can lead to a shared confirmation bias, where the group reinforces each other's beliefs and experiences, even if they are not based in reality.

It is important to note that confirmation bias is not unique to the use of Ouija boards, and can affect a wide range of beliefs and behaviors. However, in the context of the Ouija board, it can contribute to a belief in the supernatural or paranormal that may not be supported by evidence or scientific inquiry.

Placebo effect:

The placebo effect is a well-known phenomenon in which the belief in a treatment or intervention can cause a person to experience a positive response, even if the treatment itself has no inherent therapeutic value. In the context of the Ouija board, the placebo effect may come into play when participants believe that the board has the power to connect them with the spirit world or provide them with insights into their lives.

For example, a person may ask a question and then attribute the movement of the planchette to some sort of supernatural force rather than acknowledging that it is their own unconscious movements that are guiding it. The belief that the board is providing genuine information or communication can create a sense of validation or relief, leading the person to feel that their concerns have been heard and addressed.

It's important to note that the placebo effect is not a guarantee and can also lead to negative outcomes. If a person believes that the Ouija board is a tool of evil or that it can invite negative energies, this can create a negative expectation that may influence their experience in a way that reinforces those beliefs. In other words, if someone goes into a Ouija board session with the expectation that they will be harmed or that the experience will be negative, this may actually cause them to feel those negative emotions or experience negative consequences.

The placebo effect is just one of many psychological factors that may contribute to a person's experience with the Ouija board, and its influence will likely depend on the individual's beliefs, expectations, and level of engagement with the process.

Fear response:

Fear is another psychological factor that can come into play when using the Ouija board. Many people may feel uneasy or even frightened about using the board, especially if they have heard stories or seen movies that depict the board as a tool for contacting malevolent spirits or demons. This fear response can trigger physiological responses such as an increased heart rate, sweating, and rapid breathing.

In some cases, fear can also lead to a heightened sense of suggestibility, which may increase the likelihood of experiencing paranormal phenomena. For example, if someone is already feeling fearful and then experiences a slight movement of the planchette on the Ouija board, they may interpret it as evidence of supernatural activity, rather than the result of the ideomotor effect or other natural explanations.

Fear can also have negative consequences when using the Ouija board. It can create a sense of vulnerability and increase the likelihood of attracting negative energies or entities. It can also lead to an increased susceptibility to suggestion, which may make it easier for someone to be led down a path of false or misleading information.

It's important to note that fear can be a natural response to the unknown or unfamiliar. If you do decide to use the Ouija board, it's important to approach it with a clear mind and an open but cautious attitude. If at any point you feel uncomfortable or overwhelmed, it's best to stop and take a break. It's also important to remember that you have control over the situation and can choose to end the session at any time.

Catharsis:

Catharsis is a psychological term that refers to the release of emotional tension through various means. In the context of the Ouija board, some people may experience a sense of relief or catharsis from expressing their innermost thoughts and feelings through the board, even if they believe they are communicating with spirits.

The Ouija board may provide a sense of anonymity and distance from personal issues, allowing people to express themselves more freely. This can lead to a sense of emotional release and a feeling of catharsis. Some people may even feel that they have received guidance or comfort from the board, which can further reinforce their belief in its supernatural powers.

It's important to note that the sense of catharsis experienced through the Ouija board is not necessarily indicative of any actual supernatural communication. Rather, it is likely the result of the ideomotor effect, priming, and confirmation bias, which can all contribute to a person's belief in the board's efficacy and power.

Relying on the Ouija board as a source of emotional release or catharsis can be dangerous. People may become addicted to the sense of control or relief they feel from using the board, which can lead to an unhealthy dependence. It's important for individuals to seek other, more healthy forms of emotional expression and support, rather than relying on the Ouija board.

Group dynamics:

Group dynamics refer to the ways in which individuals interact and influence each other within a group setting. In the context of the Ouija board, group dynamics can play a significant role in the experience and outcome of the session.

One way in which group dynamics can affect the Ouija board experience is through conformity. People tend to conform to group norms and expectations, even if those norms conflict with their personal beliefs or experiences. This can lead to the Ouija board users conforming to the beliefs and expectations of the group, even if it goes against their own intuition or experience with the board.

Group dynamics can also create a sense of social pressure to produce results. If one or more members of the group express a desire to communicate with spirits or receive messages, it can create an expectation for the Ouija board to produce results. This pressure can cause users to interpret any movement of the planchette as a message, even if it is just random movement.

Group dynamics can create a sense of collective consciousness or energy. When a group of people focuses their attention and intention on a specific task, it can create a collective energy that can affect the outcome. In the context of the Ouija board, this collective energy can influence the movement of the planchette, even if it is not consciously intended by the users.

Group dynamics can influence the interpretation of the messages received through the Ouija board. If one member of the group interprets a message in a certain way, it can influence the interpretation of the other members. This can lead to a shared belief or understanding of the message, even if it may be unclear or ambiguous.

Group dynamics can play a significant role in the Ouija board experience and should be considered when analyzing the psychological effects of using the board.

Dissociation:

Dissociation is another psychological phenomenon that may be involved in Ouija board experiences. Dissociation is a feeling of being disconnected from one's surroundings, thoughts, and emotions. It is often described as a feeling of being "in a daze" or "in a dream." Dissociation can be triggered by traumatic events, but it can also occur in response to stress or anxiety.

When individuals use the Ouija board, they may enter into a dissociative state in which they feel detached from reality and may be more susceptible to the ideomotor effect and priming. This dissociative state may be similar to the experience of trance or hypnosis, in which the individual is highly suggestible and may experience alterations in perception or memory.

In some cases, individuals who use the Ouija board may report feeling as though they are not in control of their movements or actions while using the board. This sense of loss of control can be distressing and may contribute to feelings of fear or anxiety associated with the Ouija board.

Research on dissociation and the Ouija board is limited, but some studies have suggested a link between dissociation and paranormal beliefs. For example, one study found that individuals who reported paranormal beliefs were more likely to report symptoms of dissociation than those who did not endorse paranormal beliefs.

The role of dissociation in Ouija board experiences remains unclear, but it may be one factor that contributes to the psychological effects of using the board.

Sensory deprivation:

Sensory deprivation is a psychological phenomenon that occurs when an individual is deprived of sensory input. This can occur through physical means, such as being placed in a dark, soundproof room, or through psychological means, such as focusing intensely on a single thought or idea. Sensory deprivation can have a profound impact on an individual's perception of reality and can lead to hallucinations, delusions, and other forms of altered consciousness.

In the context of the Ouija board, sensory deprivation may play a role in the perceived supernatural experiences that users report. When using the Ouija board, participants often sit in a darkened room and focus intently on the board and planchette, while ignoring external stimuli. This prolonged focus on a single activity, combined with the lack of sensory input, can lead to dissociative experiences, where individuals feel disconnected from their surroundings and experience a sense of unreality.

The use of the planchette to communicate with unseen entities can be seen as a form of autohypnosis, where the user becomes highly suggestible and open to receiving messages from the subconscious or external sources. This suggestibility can lead to the creation of vivid mental images and sensory experiences, which may be interpreted as supernatural in nature.

It is worth noting that sensory deprivation is not always a negative experience, and can in fact be used therapeutically to induce relaxation and promote introspection. However, when combined with the suggestion and belief in supernatural forces that is often present during Ouija board sessions, sensory deprivation may contribute to the reported paranormal experiences.

Trauma:

Trauma is another psychological factor that can influence an individual's experience with the Ouija board. Trauma refers to a distressing event that has a profound and lasting effect on a person's mental and emotional well-being. Traumatic experiences can include abuse, violence, natural disasters, accidents, or other events that cause intense fear, helplessness, or horror.

For individuals who have experienced trauma, the Ouija board may trigger feelings of anxiety, fear, or even panic. This is because the experience of using the board can be reminiscent of the feelings of powerlessness and vulnerability that often accompany traumatic events.

Trauma can also affect an individual's beliefs and perceptions of the world around them. For example, someone who has experienced severe trauma may have a heightened sense of the supernatural or the paranormal. This can influence their interpretation of the Ouija board's messages and their overall experience with the board.

It is important to note that the Ouija board should not be used as a form of therapy for individuals who have experienced trauma. Instead, seeking the guidance of a mental health professional trained in trauma-focused therapies is recommended. Engaging in therapy can help individuals process and cope with their traumatic experiences in a safe and supportive environment, and may reduce the potential for negative effects associated with using the Ouija board.

The role of suggestibility and the power of suggestion in Ouija board sessions

Suggestibility refers to the tendency to accept and believe information that is presented, even if it is not true or accurate. It can play a significant role in Ouija board sessions, as participants may be more open to the possibility of receiving messages from the spirit world and may be more willing to accept any information that is provided.

The power of suggestion is also a key factor in Ouija board sessions. This refers to the ability of one person to influence the beliefs or actions of another person through suggestion or persuasion. In the context of Ouija board sessions, it may involve one participant suggesting certain questions or topics to ask the board, or even influencing the movements of the planchette.

Research has shown that suggestibility and the power of suggestion can have a significant impact on the outcomes of Ouija board sessions. In one study, participants were asked to use a Ouija board and were given false information about the identity of the spirits they were communicating with. Despite the fact that the information was clearly incorrect, many participants continued to believe in the authenticity of the communication.

The power of suggestion can also lead to the creation of false memories or beliefs. For example, a participant may believe that they received a message from a deceased loved one through the Ouija board, even if the message was fabricated by another participant or their own subconscious.

It is important to note that suggestibility and the power of suggestion are not unique to Ouija board sessions and can occur in many different contexts. However, they may be particularly potent in the context of Ouija board sessions due to the belief in the supernatural and the perceived ability to communicate with the dead.

It is important to approach Ouija board sessions with a critical and skeptical mindset and to be aware of the potential influence of suggestibility and the power of suggestion.

The potential psychological harm of using the Ouija board

While some people may have positive or neutral experiences using the Ouija board, there are also potential risks for psychological harm. Here are some ways that using the Ouija board can be psychologically harmful:

Belief in supernatural forces:

Belief in supernatural forces is a key factor that influences the potential psychological harm of using the Ouija board. When people use the board, they often believe that they are communicating with spirits or entities from the other side.

This belief can lead them to attribute their experiences to supernatural causes, rather than psychological or emotional ones.

Research has shown that belief in paranormal phenomena is associated with a range of psychological factors, including cognitive distortions, anxiety, and suggestibility. This suggests that people who believe in the supernatural may be more vulnerable to the potential negative effects of using the Ouija board.

Belief in supernatural forces can also create a sense of powerlessness and vulnerability in people. They may feel that they are at the mercy of supernatural entities, and that they have no control over their experiences. This can lead to feelings of fear, anxiety, and even paranoia.
In some cases, people may become obsessed with the Ouija board and its supposed powers. This obsession can lead to a loss of perspective and a distorted view of reality. People may begin to see everything through the lens of the board, and may become convinced that their experiences are evidence of a larger, supernatural reality.

Belief in supernatural forces can make it difficult for people to seek help or support when they experience psychological distress. They may feel that their experiences are not understood or taken seriously by others who do not share their beliefs.

Belief in supernatural forces can increase the potential psychological harm of using the Ouija board. It can create a sense of powerlessness and vulnerability, and may lead to obsessive and distorted thinking patterns. It is important for people to be aware of these potential risks before using the board, and to seek help if they experience psychological distress as a result of their experiences.

Disrupting personal beliefs:

Using the Ouija board can sometimes result in a disruption of personal beliefs. For instance, a person who has always believed in the power of positive thinking and manifestation may become confused and disheartened if they use the board and are met with negative or harmful messages. Similarly, a person who has always believed in the existence of a benevolent God or higher power may question their faith if they use the board and are met with messages that contradict their beliefs.

In some cases, the board may even encourage people to abandon their existing beliefs and adopt new, potentially harmful ones. For example, a person who uses the board and receives messages that they interpret as coming from a deceased loved one may become convinced that the board is the only way to communicate with the dead. This belief may then lead them to reject other, more established methods of communicating with the deceased, such as prayer or meditation.

The board may cause people to question their own abilities and intuition. If a person repeatedly receives messages that contradict their own beliefs or experiences, they may begin to doubt their own judgment and decision-making abilities. This can lead to feelings of confusion, anxiety, and a loss of self-confidence.

In extreme cases, the board may even lead to the development of delusional thinking or psychosis. This is especially true for people who have pre-existing mental health conditions or a history of trauma. The board's ability to tap into the user's subconscious may cause them to become convinced that they are receiving messages from supernatural forces, even when there is no evidence to support this belief. This can be dangerous and potentially harmful, as it may lead the person to make decisions or take actions that are not based in reality.

Experiencing negative emotions:

When participating in Ouija board sessions, individuals may experience a wide range of emotions, including fear, anxiety, and unease. These negative emotions can be attributed to a number of factors, including the belief that the board is connecting with malevolent spirits or the fear of the unknown.
Some individuals may also experience a sense of loss of control during the Ouija board session, as they feel as though an external force is directing their actions

and thoughts. This loss of control can lead to feelings of vulnerability and insecurity.

Some individuals may become obsessed or preoccupied with the Ouija board, leading to an increase in negative emotions such as anxiety and fear. This obsession can disrupt daily life and cause distress for individuals and their loved ones.

The potential for negative emotional experiences during and after Ouija board sessions is a significant concern, and individuals should carefully consider the potential risks before engaging in such activities. It is important to prioritize emotional safety and well-being above any perceived benefits of using the Ouija board.

Re-experiencing past traumas:

Using a Ouija board can also lead to re-experiencing past traumas. Trauma survivors may use the board as a way to connect with deceased loved ones or to find closure, but in the process, they may inadvertently trigger traumatic memories or emotions. This can lead to intense distress, anxiety, and even post-traumatic stress disorder (PTSD) symptoms.

If a participant has experienced abuse or trauma related to spiritual practices, using the Ouija board can serve as a trigger for those memories and emotions. This can be especially harmful if the individual is not prepared for or aware of the potential triggers.

It's important to note that trauma survivors should seek out professional help from a trained therapist or counselor rather than relying on the Ouija board as a means of healing or closure. Revisiting past traumas in a safe and controlled environment, under the guidance of a mental health professional, is crucial for effective healing and recovery.

The potential for re-experiencing past traumas through the use of a Ouija board highlights the need for caution and sensitivity when using any tool that could potentially trigger traumatic memories or emotions. It's important to prioritize one's own emotional and mental well-being above any perceived benefits of using the board.

Misinterpreting or exaggerating experiences:

Misinterpreting or exaggerating experiences is another potential psychological harm of using the Ouija board. When using the board, participants may interpret their experiences as communication with spirits, even if there is a logical explanation for what is happening. This can be due to suggestibility, confirmation bias, and the ideomotor effect.

For example, a participant may feel a slight movement in the planchette and interpret it as a spirit's response, even if it was caused by unintentional muscle movements or the board's surface not being completely flat. Additionally, participants may exaggerate their experiences to fit their expectations or the expectations of others, leading to a distorted perception of reality.

These misinterpretations and exaggerations can lead to false beliefs and reinforce the belief in the supernatural, which can have long-lasting psychological effects. Believing in supernatural forces can lead to feelings of powerlessness, anxiety, and even paranoia. In extreme cases, it can even lead to delusions or psychosis.

Misinterpreting or exaggerating experiences during Ouija board sessions can also disrupt the participants' ability to accurately interpret their thoughts and feelings. This can make it difficult to distinguish between their own thoughts and the supposed messages from the board. It can also lead to confusion and difficulty processing emotions, which can lead to additional psychological harm.

It is essential to recognize the potential for misinterpreting or exaggerating experiences when using the Ouija board and to approach the board with a healthy dose of skepticism and critical thinking. It is also important to seek professional help if any psychological harm is experienced as a result of using the board.

Reinforcing negative beliefs or stereotypes:

One potential psychological harm of using the Ouija board is that it can reinforce negative beliefs or stereotypes. For example, if someone has pre-existing beliefs that certain groups of people or cultures are inherently evil or associated with the supernatural, the Ouija board may provide a supposed confirmation of those beliefs through its responses.

This can be particularly harmful because it can perpetuate harmful stereotypes and biases, and can also fuel paranoia and mistrust of others. Additionally, it can contribute to a closed-minded and narrow perspective on the world, as the individual may become more resistant to evidence or information that challenges their preconceived beliefs.

The Ouija board may also reinforce negative beliefs or stereotypes about oneself. If the board consistently provides negative or critical responses, the individual may start to internalize those messages and develop negative self-perceptions.

It's important to note that these negative effects may be amplified in vulnerable or impressionable individuals, such as those with pre-existing mental health conditions or those going through a difficult time in their lives.

Reinforcing delusional beliefs:

In some cases, using the Ouija board can reinforce delusional beliefs. For example, if someone is experiencing symptoms of a mental health disorder such as schizophrenia or psychosis, they may interpret Ouija board experiences as confirmation of their delusions or hallucinations. This can lead to a reinforcement of their false beliefs and potentially worsen their condition.

If someone already has a preconceived belief in the supernatural or paranormal, the use of the Ouija board may further reinforce those beliefs, potentially leading to an over-reliance on supernatural explanations for events in their life. This can be problematic as it may prevent the individual from seeking more evidence-based explanations and treatment for their problems.

It's important to note that the Ouija board itself is not inherently dangerous, but rather the beliefs and perceptions surrounding its use can lead to potentially harmful consequences.

It is important to note that the psychological risks of using the Ouija board are not limited to these examples, and the severity of these risks may vary depending on the individual and their personal history and beliefs. It is always important to approach the use of the Ouija board with caution and mindfulness of potential psychological harm.

Chapter 7: The history of Ouija board controversy

This part delves into the history of controversy surrounding the Ouija board, which has been the subject of criticism and scrutiny since its introduction. From religious objections to claims of fraud and deceit, the Ouija board has been a lightning rod for controversy, often dividing opinion between those who believe it to be a harmless game and those who see it as a dangerous tool for connecting with the supernatural. This chapter will explore the various controversies surrounding the Ouija board and the impact they have had on its perception in popular culture.

The Ouija board and its association with demonic possession

Throughout history, the Ouija board has been linked to demonic possession, evil spirits, and satanic rituals. Many religious groups and individuals view the board as a tool of the devil and strongly discourage its use. The belief in demonic possession has been a part of many cultures for centuries, and the Ouija board has become associated with this phenomenon due to its purported ability to open a portal to the spirit world.

The idea that the Ouija board can lead to demonic possession has been popularized in movies, books, and television shows. One of the most famous examples is the 1973 horror movie "The Exorcist," which features a young girl who becomes possessed by a demon after using a Ouija board.

Some people who have claimed to experience demonic possession after using the Ouija board have reported feeling a presence or force that was not of this world. They may have also experienced physical symptoms such as nausea, headaches, and trembling. However, it is important to note that there is no scientific evidence to support the idea that the Ouija board can cause demonic possession or any other supernatural phenomenon.

Despite the lack of scientific evidence, the belief in the connection between the Ouija board and demonic possession persists in some religious circles. Many religious leaders and organizations strongly discourage the use of the board and warn their followers of the potential dangers it may pose to their spiritual well-being.

The Satanic Panic and the Ouija board

During the 1980s and early 1990s, a phenomenon known as the "Satanic Panic" swept across the United States and other parts of the world. This moral panic was characterized by a widespread belief that a network of Satan-worshipping cults was operating within society, engaging in ritual abuse, child abduction, and even human sacrifice. The Ouija board was often implicated in these alleged Satanic rituals and practices, and was seen as a gateway to demonic possession.

This belief was fueled by sensational media coverage of supposed Satanic cult activity, as well as the publication of books like Michelle Remembers and The Devil's Web, which claimed to be non-fiction accounts of Satanic cults and their practices. In many cases, individuals who reported experiencing or witnessing Satanic rituals and abuse were later found to have made false claims, sometimes under the influence of suggestive therapists or other authority figures.

Despite the lack of empirical evidence supporting the existence of widespread Satanic cults or the use of the Ouija board in such practices, the Satanic Panic had a significant impact on society. It led to the imprisonment of innocent people, the destruction of families, and the stigmatization of certain religious and cultural practices. Today, the Satanic Panic is largely viewed as a moral panic and a cautionary tale about the dangers of mass hysteria and moral fervor.

The role of the media in shaping public opinion of the Ouija board

The media has played a significant role in shaping public opinion of the Ouija board throughout history. In the late 1800s and early 1900s, newspapers often reported stories about the Ouija board being used for entertainment at social gatherings and parties. These articles generally presented the Ouija board in a positive light, describing it as a harmless parlor game.

However, in the mid-20th century, the media began to report stories about the Ouija board that portrayed it in a more negative light. In the 1970s and 1980s, during the height of the "Satanic Panic," the media often linked the Ouija board to demonic possession and other supernatural phenomena. This coverage helped to cement the Ouija board's reputation as a potentially dangerous tool for communicating with the spirit world.

Today, the Ouija board is often featured in horror movies and TV shows, which further reinforces its association with the supernatural and the occult. This portrayal in popular media has undoubtedly played a role in shaping public opinion of the Ouija board and contributing to its ongoing controversy.

here is a list of the Ouija board being featured in popular TV shows, horror movies, and books:

1. The Exorcist (1973) - This horror movie features a young girl who becomes possessed by a demon after using a Ouija board to communicate with her deceased father.

2. Witchboard (1986) - This horror movie revolves around a group of friends who use a Ouija board to communicate with a spirit, but inadvertently summon an evil entity instead.

3. Are You Afraid of the Dark? (1990-2000) - This TV show for kids features several episodes that revolve around the use of a Ouija board to communicate with spirits.

4. Paranormal Activity (2007) - This found-footage horror movie features a couple who set up a Ouija board in their home in an attempt to communicate with a spirit.

5. Ouija (2014) - This horror movie centers around a group of friends who use a Ouija board to communicate with a deceased friend, but end up summoning an evil spirit instead.

6. The Haunting of Hill House (2018) - This TV show features a family who experiences supernatural events in their haunted house, including the use of a Ouija board.

7. The Chilling Adventures of Sabrina (2018-2020) - This TV show features a group of teenage witches who use a Ouija board to communicate with spirits.

8. The Midnight Game (2013) - This horror movie revolves around a group of friends who play the "Midnight Game," which involves using a Ouija board to summon a spirit.

9. The Ouija Experiment (2011) - This horror movie features a group of friends who use a Ouija board to communicate with a spirit, but end up summoning a demonic entity instead.

10. The Omen (1976) - This horror movie features a couple who use a Ouija board to communicate with their deceased son, but end up summoning a demon instead.

11. The Uninvited (2009) - This horror movie features a group of friends who use a Ouija board to communicate with a deceased classmate, but end up uncovering a dark secret instead.

12. Stranger Things (2016-2019) - This TV show features a group of kids who use a homemade Ouija board to communicate with a missing friend.

13. The Conjuring (2013) - This horror movie features a family who experiences supernatural events in their home, including the use of a Ouija board to communicate with spirits.

14. Veronica (2017) - This Spanish horror movie features a teenage girl who uses a Ouija board to communicate with her deceased father, but ends up being haunted by a demonic entity instead.

15. The Possession (2012) - This horror movie features a young girl who becomes possessed by a dybbuk (a malevolent spirit) after playing with a Ouija board.

Many of these movies and TV shows play on the idea that using a Ouija board can lead to demonic possession or other negative consequences. However, it's important to remember that these are works of fiction and should not be taken as factual representations of the Ouija board or its effects.

Chapter 8: Other divination methods and their comparison with the Ouija board

Divination has been used throughout history as a means of obtaining information about the future or the unknown. While the Ouija board is one of the most well-known and controversial divination tools, it is not the only one. This chapter will examine some of the other divination methods such as tarot cards, crystal balls, pendulums, and automatic writing. We will explore the similarities and differences between these methods and the Ouija board, including their history, cultural significance, and potential for psychological and spiritual effects.

An overview of other divination methods, such as tarot cards, astrology, and palm reading

 In addition to the Ouija board, there are a variety of other divination methods that have been used throughout history to gain insight into the future or access hidden knowledge. Some of the most well-known divination methods include tarot cards, astrology, and palm reading.

Tarot cards are a deck of 78 cards that are typically used to gain insight into personal matters, such as love, career, and spirituality. Each card has a unique symbol or image, and a skilled reader can interpret the cards based on their position in a spread and the relationships between them.

Astrology, on the other hand, is a system that uses the positions and movements of celestial bodies to gain insight into personality traits, relationships, and future events. Astrology is based on the belief that the positions of the planets at the time of a person's birth can influence their personality and life path.

Palm reading, also known as palmistry, involves the interpretation of the lines and markings on a person's palm to gain insight into their character and future. A skilled palm reader can analyze the length, depth, and shape of the lines on the palm to make predictions about a person's life.

While these divination methods differ in their specific techniques and tools, they share a common goal of providing insight into the unknown. In the following sections, we will explore these divination methods in more detail and compare them to the Ouija board.

The similarities and differences between these methods and the Ouija board

let's explore the similarities and differences between the Ouija board and other divination methods:

Similarities:

- All these methods are used for divination, which means attempting to gain insight into the future or the unknown through supernatural means.

- They all involve some level of interpretation or reading of symbols, whether it's interpreting the movements of a planchette on a Ouija board, interpreting the images on tarot cards, or interpreting the lines on a palm.

- They are all used as tools for self-reflection and introspection, helping people gain insight into their own lives and potential paths.

Differences:

- The Ouija board is unique in that it involves communication with a spirit or entity, whereas tarot cards, astrology, and palm reading are more focused on personal reflection and self-exploration.

- Tarot cards, for example, offer a more structured approach to divination, with a set of cards with specific meanings and interpretations, whereas the Ouija board is more freeform and open-ended.

- Astrology involves the interpretation of the position and movement of celestial bodies, while palm reading involves the interpretation of the lines on an individual's palm.

- The level of belief and acceptance of these methods varies among different cultures and individuals.

While all these divination methods may have some similarities, they are distinct in their practices, beliefs, and cultural significance. It's up to each individual to decide which method resonates with them the most.

Why people choose the Ouija board over other divination methods

There are several reasons why people may choose to use the Ouija board over other divination methods. One of the main reasons is its ease of use - unlike tarot cards or astrology, which require extensive knowledge and training to interpret, the Ouija board is relatively straightforward to use.
Additionally, the Ouija board allows for direct communication with spirits, while other divination methods may only offer insight or guidance.

Some people may also be drawn to the Ouija board because of its reputation for being a powerful tool for connecting with the supernatural. The board has been featured in numerous horror movies and TV shows, which may add to its allure and mystique.

It's worth noting that some people may choose to use multiple divination methods, including the Ouija board, in order to gain a more complete understanding of their situation or to verify information received through another method. Ultimately, the choice of divination method often comes down to personal preference and belief system.

Chapter 9: Conclusion and recommendations

its history, controversy, and psychology. In this chapter, we'll summarize the key points and findings discussed throughout the book and offer some recommendations for those interested in using the Ouija board or other divination methods.

Throughout the book, we've examined the Ouija board from various perspectives, including its history, religious and cultural beliefs, psychological effects, and media portrayal.

We've discussed how the Ouija board is often associated with the supernatural, including beliefs in spirits, ghosts, and demonic possession. We've also explored the psychological mechanisms that may be at play during Ouija board sessions, such as priming, ideomotor effect, and suggestibility.

In addition to the Ouija board, we've also looked at other divination methods, such as tarot cards, astrology, and palm reading, and compared their similarities and differences to the Ouija board.

Now, in this final chapter, we'll offer some recommendations for those who are interested in using the Ouija board or other divination methods, as well as some key takeaways from our exploration of this fascinating and controversial tool.

A summary of the book's main points

Throughout the book, we have explored various aspects of the Ouija board, including its history, cultural significance, psychological effects, controversy, and comparison with other divination methods.

First, we looked at the history of the Ouija board, tracing its origins back to spiritualism in the 19th century and its commercialization in the early 20th century. We also explored its cultural significance in different religions and spiritual practices.

Next, we examined the psychological effects of using the Ouija board, such as priming, ideomotor effect, confirmation bias, fear response, catharsis, group dynamics, dissociation, and sensory deprivation. We discussed how these factors can contribute to users' experiences and perceptions of the board.

We also examined the potential psychological harm of using the Ouija board, such as reinforcing negative beliefs and stereotypes, disrupting personal beliefs, experiencing negative emotions, re-experiencing past traumas, misinterpreting or exaggerating experiences, and reinforcing delusional beliefs.

We delved into the controversies surrounding the Ouija board, such as its association with demonic possession, the Satanic Panic, and the role of the media in shaping public opinion.

We compared the Ouija board with other divination methods, such as tarot cards, astrology, and palm reading. We discussed the similarities and differences between these methods and the Ouija board, as well as why people choose the Ouija board over other divination methods.

This book provides a comprehensive exploration of the Ouija board and its various aspects, offering insights and recommendations for those interested in using or studying this controversial divination tool.

Personal recommendations for readers who are considering using the Ouija board

here are some personal recommendations for readers who are considering using the Ouija board:

Understand the risks:

Before using the Ouija board, it is important to understand the potential risks and negative consequences that can come with it. This includes the possibility of negative psychological effects, reinforcing delusional beliefs, and the potential for harm if used incorrectly or with ill intentions.

Consider alternative divination methods:

While the Ouija board can be a popular and intriguing divination tool, there are many other methods available such as tarot cards, astrology, and palm reading. It may be worth exploring these options before deciding to use the Ouija board.

Approach with caution:

If you do decide to use the Ouija board, approach it with caution and respect. It is important to set clear intentions, create a safe and comfortable environment, and be mindful of your own emotions and reactions during the session.

Seek guidance:

If you are new to using the Ouija board or have concerns about its use, it may be helpful to seek guidance from an experienced practitioner or spiritual advisor.

Trust your intuition:

Ultimately, trust your own intuition and feelings about whether or not using the Ouija board is the right choice for you. Listen to your own inner guidance and make decisions that align with your values and beliefs.

Final thoughts on the controversy surrounding the Ouija board

The Ouija board has been a controversial topic for over a century, with many people expressing strong opinions both for and against its use. While some see it as a harmless game or tool for divination, others view it as a dangerous portal to the spirit world that should be avoided at all costs.

After exploring the history, psychology, and potential risks of using the Ouija board, it is clear that there is no one-size-fits-all answer to the question of whether or not it should be used.
Ultimately, it is up to each individual to make an informed decision based on their own beliefs, experiences, and comfort level.

However, it is important to keep in mind that any activity that involves attempting to communicate with supernatural forces can carry risks, both physical and psychological. It is crucial to approach such activities with caution, to have a clear understanding of the potential risks involved, and to take steps to minimize those risks as much as possible.

Regardless of one's personal beliefs about the Ouija board, it is important to approach the topic with an open mind and a willingness to engage in thoughtful, respectful discussion with those who may hold different perspectives. By doing so, we can continue to learn and grow, both individually and as a society.

In conclusion, this book has provided a comprehensive exploration of the Ouija board and its cultural significance, as well as its potential psychological and spiritual implications. The history of the Ouija board has been traced, from its early development as a parlor game to its later association with the occult and demonic possession. The controversy surrounding the Ouija board has been examined, with a particular focus on the role of the media in shaping public opinion.

The potential psychological and spiritual effects of using the Ouija board have been discussed, including the role of suggestibility and belief in supernatural forces, as well as the potential for reinforcing negative beliefs or stereotypes and re-experiencing past traumas. Other divination methods, such as tarot cards, astrology, and palm reading, have been compared and contrasted with the Ouija board.

Throughout the book, the authors have emphasized the importance of critical thinking and personal responsibility when it comes to engaging with the Ouija board or any other divination method. While some may find the use of the Ouija board to be a harmless form of entertainment, others may experience negative psychological or spiritual effects.
Ultimately, the decision to use the Ouija board or any other divination method should be made with careful consideration and respect for one's own beliefs and boundaries.

Printed in Great Britain
by Amazon